Hiking Anza-Borrego Desert State Park

Help Us Keep This Guide Up to Date

Every effort has been made by the authors and editors to make this guide as accurate and use-ful as possible. However, many things can change after a guide is published—trails are rerouted, regulations change, techniques evolve, facilities come under new management, etc.

We would love to hear from you concerning your experiences with this guide and how you feel it could be improved and kept up to date. While we may not be able to respond to all com-ments and suggestions, we'll take them to heart, and we'll also make certain to share them with the authors. Please send your comments and suggestions to the following address:

> The Globe Pequot Press
> Reader Response/Editorial Department
> P.O. Box 480
> Guilford, CT 06437

Or you may e-mail us at:

> editorial@GlobePequot.com

Thanks for your input, and happy trails!

Hiking Anza-Borrego Desert State Park

25 Day and Overnight Hikes

Bill and Polly Cunningham

FALCONGUIDES ®

GUILFORD, CONNECTICUT
HELENA, MONTANA
AN IMPRINT OF THE GLOBE PEQUOT PRESS

FALCONGUIDES®

Falcon and FalconGuides are registered trademarks of
Morris Book Publishing, LLC.

Text design by Nancy Freeborn
Maps created by XNR Productions Inc. © Morris Book
Publishing, LLC
All interior photos by Polly and Bill Cunningham

Library of Congress Cataloging-in-Publication Data
Cunningham, Bill, 1943–
  Hiking Anza-Borrego Desert State Park/Bill and Polly
  Cunningham. — 1st ed.
    p. cm.
  Includes index.
  ISBN 978-0-7627-4462-6
  1. Hiking—California—Anza-Borrego Desert State Park—
  Guidebooks. 2. Anza-Borrego Desert State Park
  (Calif.)—Guidebooks. I. Cunningham, Polly. II. Title.
  GV199.42.C22A5925 2006
  796.5109794—dc22
                                        2006026137

Manufactured in the United States of America
First Edition/First Printing

To buy books in quantity for corporate use
or incentives, call **(800) 962–0973**
or e-mail **premiums@GlobePequot.com**.

To the thousands of citizens from California and elsewhere, past and present, who laid the groundwork for protection of a large portion of the California desert and to the dedicated state and federal park rangers and naturalists charged with stewardship of California's irreplaceable desert wilderness.

Contents

Acknowledgments

This book could not have been written without the generous assistance of knowledgeable park staff. Special thanks to Homer Townsend, chief ranger, and Mark Jorgensen, associate resource ecologist at Anza-Borrego Desert State Park. Kathy Dice, supervising state park ranger, also deserves special recognition. Kathy circulated our request for updated information to her rangers and forwarded a mountain of useful information back to us. Her enthusiasm and love for Anza-Borrego are especially appreciated.

Our thanks also to all the hospitable folks who provided advice and insights during our treks in the desert. Please know that you are not forgotten.

Thanks to you all!

Introduction

The California desert covers the southeastern quarter of our most populous and most ecologically diverse state. Incredibly, three of the four desert subregions that make up most of the arid southwest corner of North America are found within the California desert. These subregions—the Colorado (called the Sonoran in Mexico), Mojave, and Great Basin Deserts—differ by climate and distinct plant and animal communities.

The geographer's definition of a desert as a place with less than 10 inches average annual rainfall says little about what a desert really is. Deserts are regions of irregular and minimal rainfall, so much so that for most of the time, scarcity of water is limiting to life. Averages mean nothing in a desert region that may go one or two years without *any* rain only to receive up to three times the annual average the following year.

In the desert, evaporation far exceeds precipitation. Temperatures swing widely between night and day. This is because low humidity and intense sun heat up the ground during the day, but almost all of the heat dissipates at night. Daily temperature changes of 50 degrees or more are common—which can be hazardous to unprepared hikers caught out after dark.

Sparse rainfall means sparse vegetation, which in turn means naked geological features. Most of the California desert is crisscrossed with mountain ranges, imparting an exposed, rough-hewn, scenic character to the landscape. Rather than having been uplifted, the mountains were largely formed by an east-west collision of the earth's tectonic plates, producing a north-south orientation of the ranges. Some would call the result stark, but all would agree that these signatures on the land are dramatic and, at times, overpowering. This very starkness tends to exaggerate the drama of space, color, relief, and sheer ruggedness.

Despite sparse plant cover, the number of individual plant species in the California desert is amazing. At least 1,000 species are spread among 103 vascular plant families. Equally amazing is the diversity of bird life and other wildlife on this deceptively barren land. Many of these birds and animals are active only at night, or are most likely seen during the hotter months at or near watering holes. Hundreds of bird species and more than sixty kinds of reptiles and amphibians fly, nest, crawl, and slither in habitat niches to which they have adapted. Desert bighorn sheep and the rare mountain lion are at the top of the charismatic mega-fauna list, but at least sixty other species of mammals make the desert their home—from kit foxes on the valley floors to squirrels on the highest mountain crests. The best way to observe these desert denizens is on foot, far from the madding crowd, in the peace and solitude of desert wilderness.

In 1933, years before the federal government took action to protect California's desert wildlands under the California Desert Protection Act of 1994, the state set aside Anza-Borrego Desert State Park within the Colorado (Sonoran) Desert, which extends deep into Arizona and Mexico. This is the hottest and lowest of the desert types, with elevations from below sea level to 4,500 feet. Temperatures are among the highest in the United States, with summer highs of 120 degrees or more. Characteristic plants include jumping cholla, creosote bushes, ocotillo, and ironwood.

Anza-Borrego is included within the Colorado and Mojave Desert Biosphere Reserve, which was internationally designated in 1984. There are more than 265 biosphere reserves worldwide that protect lands within each of the earth's biogeographic regions. The park is within the core of the biosphere reserve, where human impact is kept to a minimum. The core is surrounded by a multiple-use area where sustainable development is the guiding principle.

Anza-Borrego and other desert parks receive many international visitors who are drawn to the desert because there is no desert in their homeland. Many come during the peak of summer to experience the desert at its hottest. Regardless of whether the visitor is from Europe, a nearby California town, or someplace across the nation, the endlessly varied desert offers something for everyone. Unlike snowbound northern regions, the California desert is a year-round hiker's paradise. There is no better place in which to actually see the raw, exposed forces of land-shaping geology at work. Those interested in history and paleoarchaeology will have a field day. And the list goes on. This book is designed to enhance the enjoyment of all who wish to sample the richness of Anza-Borrego Desert State Park on their own terms. Travel is best done on foot, with distance and destination being far less important than the experience of getting there.

Have Fun and Be Safe

Wandering in the desert has a reputation of being a dangerous activity, thanks to both the Bible and Hollywood. Usually depicted as a wasteland, the desert evokes fear. With proper planning, however, desert hiking is not hazardous. In fact, it is fun and exciting and is quite safe.

An enjoyable desert outing requires preparation. Beginning with this book, along with the maps suggested in the hike write-ups, you need to be equipped with adequate knowledge about your hiking area. Carry good maps and a compass, and know how to use them.

Calculating the time required for a hike in the desert defies any formula. Terrain is often rough; extensive detours around boulders, dry falls, and drop-offs mean longer trips. Straight-line distance is an illusion. Sun, heat, and wind likewise all conspire to slow down even the speediest hiker. Therefore, distances are not what they appear in the desert. Five desert miles may take longer than 10 woodland miles. Plan your excursion conservatively, and always carry emergency items in your pack (see appendix B).

While you consult the equipment list (appendix B), note that water ranks the highest. Carrying the water is not enough—take the time to stop and drink it. This is another reason desert hikes take longer. Frequent water breaks are mandatory. It's best to return from your hike with empty water bottles. You can cut down on loss of bodily moisture by hiking with your mouth closed and breathing through your nose; reduce thirst also by avoiding sweets and alcohol.

Driving to and from the trailhead is statistically far more dangerous than hiking in the desert backcountry. But being far from the nearest 911 service requires knowledge about possible hazards and proper precautions to avoid them. It is not an oxymoron to have fun and to be safe. Quite to the contrary: If you're not safe, you won't have fun. At the risk of creating excessive paranoia, here are the treacherous twelve:

Dehydration

It cannot be overemphasized that plenty of water is necessary for desert hiking. Carry one gallon per person per day in unbreakable plastic screw-top containers. And pause often to drink it. Carry water in your car as well so you'll have water to return to. As a general rule, plain water is a better thirst-quencher than any of the colored fluids on the market, which usually generate greater thirst. It is very important to maintain proper electrolyte balance by eating small quantities of nutritional foods throughout the day, even if you feel you don't have an appetite.

Changeable Weather

The desert is well known for sudden changes in the weather. The temperature can change 50 degrees in less than an hour. Prepare yourself with extra food and clothing, rain/wind gear, and a flashlight. When leaving on a trip, let someone know your exact route, especially if traveling solo, and your estimated time of return; don't forget to let them know when you get back. Register your route at the closest park office or backcountry board, especially for longer hikes that involve cross-country travel.

Hypothermia/Hyperthermia

Abrupt chilling is as much a danger in the desert as heat stroke. Storms and/or nightfall can cause desert temperatures to plunge. Wear layers of clothes, adding or subtracting depending on conditions, to avoid overheating or chilling. At the other extreme, you need to protect yourself from sun and wind with proper clothing. The broad-brimmed hat is mandatory equipment for the desert traveler. Even in the cool days of winter, a delightful time in the desert, the sun's rays are intense.

Vegetation

You quickly will learn not to come in contact with certain desert vegetation. Catclaw, Spanish bayonet, and cacti are just a few of the botanical hazards that will get your attention if you become complacent. Carry tweezers to extract cactus spines. Wear long pants if traveling off-trail or in a brushy area. Many folks carry a hair comb to assist with removal of cholla balls.

Rattlesnakes, Scorpions, Tarantulas

These desert "creepy crawlies" are easily terrified by unexpected human visitors, and they react predictably to being frightened. Do not sit or put your hands in dark places you can't see, especially during the warmer "snake season" months. Carry and know how to use your snakebite-venom-extractor kit for emergencies when help is far away. In the event of a snakebite, seek medical assistance as quickly as possible.

Keep tents zipped and always shake out boots, packs, and clothes before putting them on.

Mountain Lions

The California desert is mountain-lion country. Avoid hiking at night, when lions are often hunting. Instruct your children on appropriate behavior when confronted with a lion. Do not run. Keep children in sight while hiking; stay close to them in areas where lions might hide.

Mine Hazards

The California desert contains thousands of deserted mines. All of them should be considered hazardous. Stay away from all mines and mine structures. The vast majority of these mines have not been secured or even posted. Keep an eye on young or adventuresome members of your group.

Hanta Virus

In addition to the mines, there are often deserted buildings around the mine sites. Hanta virus is a deadly disease carried by deer mice in the Southwest. Any enclosed area increases the chances of breathing the airborne particles that carry this life-threatening virus. As a precaution, do not enter deserted buildings.

Flash Floods

Desert washes and canyons can become traps for unwary visitors when rainstorms hit the desert. Keep a watchful eye on the sky. Never camp in flash-flood areas. Check at a ranger station on regional weather conditions before embarking on your back-country expedition. A storm anywhere upstream in a drainage can result in a sudden torrent in a lower canyon. Do not cross a flooded wash. Both the depth and the current can be deceiving; wait for the flood to recede, which usually does not take long.

Lightning

Be aware of lightning, especially during summer storms. Stay off ridges and peaks. Shallow overhangs and gullies should also be avoided because electrical current often moves at ground level near a lightning strike.

Unstable Rocky Slopes

Desert canyons and mountainsides often consist of crumbly or fragmented rock. Mountain sheep are better adapted to this terrain than us bipeds. Use caution when climbing; the downward journey is usually the more hazardous. Smooth rock faces such as in slickrock canyons are equally dangerous, especially when you've got sand on the soles of your boots. On those rare occasions when they are wet, the rocks are slicker than ice.

Giardia

Any surface water, with the possible exception of springs where they flow out of the ground, is apt to contain *Giardia lamblia,* a microorganism that causes severe diarrhea. Boil water for at least five minutes or use a filter system. Iodine drops are not effective in killing this pesky parasite.

Zero-Impact Desert Etiquette

The desert environment is fragile; damage lasts for decades—even centuries. Desert courtesy requires us to leave no evidence that we were ever there. This ethic means no grafitti or defoliation at one end of the spectrum, and no unnecessary footprints on delicate vegetation on the other. Here are seven general guidelines for desert wilderness behavior:

Avoid making new trails. If hiking cross-country, stay on one set of footprints when traveling in a group. Try to make your route invisible. Desert vegetation grows very slowly. Its destruction leads to wind and water erosion and irreparable harm to the desert. Darker crusty soil that crumbles easily indicates cryptogamic soils, which are a living blend of tightly bonded mosses, lichens, and bacteria. This dark crust prevents wind and water erosion and protects seeds that fall into the soil. Walking can destroy this fragile layer. Take special care to avoid stepping on cryptogamic soil.

Keep noise down. Desert wilderness means quiet and solitude, for the animal life as well as other human visitors.

Leave your pets at home. Check with park authorities before including your dog in the group. Better yet, share other experiences with your best friend, not the desert.

Pack it in/pack it out. This is more true in the desert than anywhere else. Desert winds spread debris, and desert air preserves it. Always carry a trash bag, both for your trash and for any that you encounter. If you must smoke, pick up your butts and bag them. Bag and carry out toilet paper (it doesn't deteriorate in the desert) and feminine hygiene products.

Never camp near water. Most desert animals are nocturnal, and most, like the bighorn sheep, are exceptionally shy. The presence of humans is very disturbing, so camping near their water source means they will go without water. Camp in already-used sites if possible to reduce further damage. If none is available, camp on ground that is already bare. And use a camp stove. Ground fires are forbidden in most desert parks; gathering wood is also not permitted. Leave your campsite as you found it. Better yet, improve it by picking up litter, cleaning out fire rings, or scattering ashes of any inconsiderate predecessors. Remember that artifacts fifty years old or older are protected by federal law and must not be moved or removed.

Treat human waste properly. Bury human waste 4 inches deep and at least 200 feet from water and trails. Pack out toilet paper and feminine hygiene products; they do not decompose in the arid desert. Do not burn toilet paper; many wildfires have been started this way.

Respect wildlife. Living in the desert is hard enough without being harassed by human intruders. Remember this is the only home these animals have. They treasure their privacy. Be respectful and use binoculars for long-distance viewing. *Especially important:* Do not molest the rare desert water sources by playing or bathing in them.

Beyond these guidelines, refer to park regulations for specific rules governing backcountry usage. Enjoy the beauty and solitude of the desert, and leave it for others to enjoy.

How to Use This Book

This guide is *the* source book for those who wish to experience on foot the very best hikes and backcountry trips Anza-Borrego Desert State Park has to offer. Hikers are given many choices from which they can pick and choose, depending on their wishes and abilities.

The maps in this book that depict a detailed close-up of an area use elevation tints, called hypsometry, to portray relief. Each gray tone represents a range of equal elevation, as shown in the scale key with the map. These maps will give you a good idea of elevation gain and loss. The darker tones are lower elevations and the lighter grays are higher elevations. The lighter the tone, the higher the elevation. Narrow bands of different gray tones spaced closely together indicate steep terrain, whereas wider bands indicate areas of more gradual slope.

Maps that show larger geographic areas use shaded, or shadow, relief. Shadow relief does not represent elevation; it demonstrates slope or relative steepness. This gives an almost 3-D perspective of the physiography of a region and will help you see where ranges and valleys are.

For a general geographic orientation, begin with the overview map in the next section. Here you'll find the relative locations of the park's hikes. The numbering of the individual hikes generally runs south to north, although this is sometimes altered by the clustering of hikes sharing common access.

Refer to the "Hikes at a Glance" matrix on page 18 for a quick overview of all of the hikes presented for the park. After making your selections, turn to the specific hike descriptions for added detail. Each hike is numbered and named and begins with a general description. This overview briefly describes the type of hike and highlights the destination and key features.

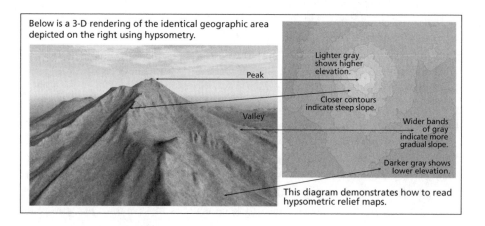

Below is a 3-D rendering of the identical geographic area depicted on the right using hypsometry.

Peak

Lighter gray shows higher elevation.

Closer contours indicate steep slope.

Valley

Wider bands of gray indicate more gradual slope.

Darker gray shows lower elevation.

This diagram demonstrates how to read hypsometric relief maps.

The "start" is the approximate road distance from a nearby town or park visitor center to the trailhead. The idea is to give you a mental picture of where the hike is in relation to your prospective travels.

Hike "distance" is given in total miles for the described route. The mileage is in one direction for a loop, in which you return to the place where you started without retracing your steps, or for a one-way hike, in which you begin at one trailhead and end at another, requiring two vehicles, a shuttle bus, or another driver to pick you up or deposit you at either end. Round-trip mileage is provided for an out-and-back hike, in which you return to the trailhead the same way you came. A lollipop loop combines a stretch of out-and-back with a loop at one end. Mileages were calculated in the field and double-checked as accurately as possible with the most detailed topographic maps.

"Approximate hiking time" provides a best guess as to how long it will take the average hiker to complete the route. Always add more time for further exploration or for contemplation.

The "difficulty" rating is necessarily subjective, but it is based on the authors' extensive backcountry experience with folks of all ages and abilities. Easy hikes present no difficulty to hikers of all abilities. Moderate hikes are challenging to inexperienced hikers and might tax even experienced hikers. Strenuous hikes are extremely difficult and challenging, even for the most-seasoned hikers. Distance, elevation gain and loss, trail condition, and terrain were considered in assigning the difficulty rating. There are, of course, many variables. The easiest hike can be sheer torture if you run out of water in extreme heat—a definite no-no.

"Trail surfaces" are evaluated based on well-defined trail standards. Dirt trails have no obstructions and are easy to follow. Rocky trails may be partially blocked by slides, rocks, or debris but are generally obvious and easy to find. Primitive trails are faint, rough, and rocky and may have disappeared completely in places. In the desert some of the best hiking takes place on old four-wheel-drive mining roads that are now closed to vehicular use because of wilderness designation or to protect key values, such as wildlife watering holes. Many of the desert hikes are off-trail in washes, canyons, ridges, and fans. "Use trails" may form a segment of the route. A use trail is simply an informal, unconstructed path created solely by the passage of hikers.

The best "season" is based largely on the moderate-temperature months for the particular hike and is greatly influenced by elevation. Additional consideration is given to seasonal road access at higher altitudes. The range of months given is not necessarily the best time for wildflowers, which is highly localized and dependent on elevation and rainfall. Nor is it necessarily the best time to view wildlife, which may be during the driest and hottest summer months near water sources.

The maps listed are the best available for route-finding and land navigation: the relevant 7.5-minute topographic map (1:24,000 scale or 2.6 inches = 1 mile) with a 40-foot contour interval. These U.S. Geological Survey maps can usually be purchased at the park visitor center. They can also be purchased for $6.00 each (price as of this writing) directly from Map Distribution, USGS Map Sales, Box 25286, Federal Center, Building 810, Denver, CO 80225; by calling (800) ASK–USGS; or online at www.usgs.gov/pubprod/. See appendix C for a listing of other useful smaller-scale maps.

For more information on the hike, the best available "trail contact" for the park management agency is listed. See appendix D for a listing of agency addresses and phone numbers.

"Finding the trailhead" includes detailed up-to-date driving instructions to the trailhead or jumping-off point for each hike. For most hikes, there is no formal trail-head but rather a starting point where you can park. To follow these instructions, start with the beginning reference point, which might be the park visitor center, a nearby town, or an important road junction. Pay close attention to mileage and land-mark instructions. American Automobile Association (AAA) map mileages are used when available, but in many instances we had to rely on our car odometer, which may vary slightly from other car odometers.

The text following the driving directions is a narrative of the actual route, with general directions and key features noted. In some cases interpretation of the natural and cultural history of the hike and its surroundings is included. The idea is to provide accurate route-finding instructions, with enough supporting information to enhance your enjoyment of the hike without diminishing your sense of discovery— a fine line indeed. Some of these descriptions are augmented with photographs that preview a representative segment of the hike.

The trail itinerary, "Miles and Directions," provides detailed mile-by-mile instructions while noting landmarks, trail junctions, canyon entrances, dry falls, peaks, and historic sites along the way.

And last, please don't allow our value-laden list of "favorite hikes" (appendix A) to discourage you from completing any of the other hikes. They're all worth doing!

Map Legend

Boundaries

	National wilderness/ preserve boundary
	National park boundary
	State park boundary
	County park boundary
— · — ··	State boundary

Transportation

15	Interstate
95	U.S. highway
62	State highway
522	Primary road
	Other road
	Unpaved road
= = = = =	Unimproved road
= = = = =	Featured unimproved road
— — — —	Featured trail
··············	Optional trail
- - - - - - -	Other trail
+—+—+—+	Railroad
·—·—·—	Power line

Hydrology

╲ ╱ ╲	Intermittent stream
ρ	Spring
∬	Fall
	Lake
	Dry lake
	Lava bed
	Sand/wash

Physiography

×	Spot elevation
)(	Pass
▲	Peak
∩	Cave
⊔⊔⊔	Cliff

Symbols

🚶	Trailhead
START	Trail start
❷	Trail locator
↻	Trail turnaround
P	Parking
🚻	Restroom/toilet
△	Campground
▲	Backcountry campground
♠	Lodging
?	Visitor center
	Ranger station
☎	Telephone
⊞	Picnic area
○	Town
👁	Overlook
▪	Point of interest
⚒	Mine/prospect
•—•	Gate
⋈	Bridge
✛ —	Airport/ landing strip

Anza-Borrego Desert State Park

A nza-Borrego Desert State Park was set aside by the state of California in 1933, decades before the state's population expanded and desert junctions grew into cities. Anza-Borrego's irregular boundary encloses 600,000 acres, making it California's largest state park, 63 percent of which is protected in twelve wilderness areas. One thousand private inholdings are located within the park; the town of Borrego Springs is an island surrounded by it. The name Anza-Borrego, adopted in 1957, is a blend of the human and natural history of the San Diego desert: *Anza* for the Spanish explorer who traversed the region with a party of emigrants in 1774, and *Borrego,* a Spanish word meaning bighorn sheep, for those animals that still make these desert mountains and canyons their home.

Ten million years ago the Anza-Borrego region formed the floor of a great inland sea. As the mountains rose and the Colorado River delta expanded, the area was eventually blocked from the sea, and the water diminished. A million years ago mastodons and saber-tooths roamed the savannahs around the receding estuary. Early man arrived in the region at least 10,000 years ago and enjoyed the temperate climate of Southern California. The rivers, lakes, and grasslands provided a bountiful environment for humans and animals. Gradual warming began 8,000 years ago. Rising mountains to the west, driven upward by faults and earthquakes as tectonic plates collided, blocked the moisture-laden oceanic winds. Ancient ice-age lakes became playas. The desert began to form.

The earth's dynamics that created the landscape at Anza-Borrego are still at work. Like many desert regions, the park is a geology lab in action. The San Andreas Fault, to the north and east of the park, is constantly shifting. Park elevations range from 15 feet near Travertine Point (northeast corner of the park) to 6,193 feet at Combs Peak in the Bucksnort Mountains on the west. Vast valleys, badlands, canyons, oases, and mountain ranges are included in this varied geological wonderland.

Natural and Human History

Animals, plants, and man adapted to a changing climate as this Southern California region became a desert. The endangered desert pupfish are well-known residents of

Native California fan palm grove at the Borrego Palm Oasis.

Anza-Borrego that date from earlier times. As the prehistoric inland sea shrank and increased in salinity, this hardy member of the minnow family adapted to the new conditions. Pupfish can live within a broad range of temperatures (from 34 to more than 108 degrees F) and in water twice as saline as seawater. Ponds at the park's visitor center and the Borrego Palm Canyon trailhead harbor pupfish schools.

Of the famed Peninsular bighorn sheep, only about 400 of these rare animals remain. Researchers are actively engaged in finding the cause of their continued decline here in the park. Three groups live in the Santa Rosa Mountains, the Vallecitos Mountains, and Carrizo Gorge, while two more herds hang out in Coyote and Palm Canyons. Hikers may spot these elusive denizens of the desert in the rocky, high backcountry. Sheep also drop down to canyon water sources every few days for an early-morning drink. They can be seen in Borrego Palm Canyon or at other streams. Because the shrunken water sources of summer put pressure on the sheep

Pond near the beginning of the Borrego Palm Canyon trail ▶
provides a sanctuary for the endangered desert pupfish.

population, Coyote Canyon is closed to all human visitors from June 1 through September 30 to protect the sheep's access to water there.

In addition to these two celebrity species, nearly 60 mammal species, 270 bird species, 27 snake species, and 31 lizard species call Anza-Borrego home, dispelling the myth that there is no life in the desert. An evening coyote chorus is evidence of a flourishing rodent food chain. It does take a sharp eye to spot desert creatures. Many are nocturnal, and most are very shy. Do not camp, therefore, within 200 yards of a water source to allow the animals a chance to drink. The twenty-five oases in the park are the most likely locations for viewing wildlife.

In the botanical kingdom, Anza-Borrego is in the Colorado (Sonoran) Desert. California fan palms *(Washingtonia filifera)*, the only palm tree native to California, are numerous at the springs and oases and in the canyons of Anza-Borrego. The rare elephant tree *(Bursera microphylla)* exists here and nowhere else in California. Chaparral vegetation dominates the higher mountains on the western side of the park. At lower elevations creosote bushes and ocotillo are common. Twenty-two varieties of cacti, especially several of the ubiquitous cholla family, flourish, ranging from the 3-inch fishhook cactus to the barrel cactus, sometimes over 8 feet tall. Removing or disturbing any of these plants is forbidden by law.

The spectacular spring bloom of desert wildflowers attracts thousands of visitors annually. The flower season ranges from late February through April, depending on the weather. Park naturalists will notify you of the anticipated peak bloom. Send a self-addressed stamped postcard to WILDFLOWERS, Anza-Borrego Desert State Park, 200 Palm Canyon Drive, Borrego Springs, CA 92004, if you would like to be notified about two weeks before the peak. The park also maintains a flower hotline, (760) 767–4684, or can be visited on the Web at www.anzaborrego.statepark.org.

Man is a relative newcomer, arriving from 6,000 to 10,000 years ago. These early inhabitants left few artifacts. They left no pottery since they stored their food in rock-lined caches. They hunted with spears, not the more advanced bow and arrow. Beginning 2,000 years ago, the Kumeyaay people from the Colorado River, and the Cahuilla people from the Great Basin, migrated to the Anza-Borrego region. These were seminomadic hunter-gatherers. Sites of their *morteros,* pictographs, and petroglyphs are numerous, as are their fire rings and fire pits, their ancient trails, campsite middens, and fragments of pottery. All artifacts are protected by law and must not be altered or removed by visitors. Please leave these traces of prior inhabitants for future generations to enjoy.

Beginning in the eighteenth century with the Anza expedition, Spanish and American groups have traveled through this desert, heading for the coastal areas of Southern California. Several historical routes of emigrants and stages can be seen in the Blair Valley and Collins Valley areas. In the late nineteenth century, ranchers and farmers began to settle in Borrego Springs and the nearby valleys. Their efforts to make the desert productive had varied results. Today stock watering tanks can be found in remote corners of the park, remnants of the defunct cattle industry, whereas

Wilson Trail leading to the northwest at mile 1.3.

the green orchards of Borrego Valley indicate greater success for the growers. Unlike the other desert parks of Southern California, Anza-Borrego was never the scene of frenzied mining activity. Mine openings and tailings do not dot the mountainsides.

How and When to Get There

Anza-Borrego Desert State Park is 80 miles east of San Diego at the eastern border of San Diego County. Interstate 8 passes by the park's southern boundary on the way to El Centro. California Highway 78 is the major access route to the central region of the park. County Road S22 is the highway to Borrego Springs, where the park visitor center is located.

The nearest commercial airports are in San Diego and Palm Springs, although an airport in Borrego Springs provides facilities for private aircraft and refueling.

Although the summer is typically sizzling in Anza-Borrego, with temperatures well over 100 degrees F, the remainder of the year features highs from 70 to 85 degrees. Average annual rainfall at park headquarters is about 6 inches, but that figure can be misleading. Winter months may bring heavy downpours. The summer months also have occasional thunderstorms. Heavy rains in any season may result in flash flooding, washouts, and road closures. Always check the park Web site before heading to Anza-Borrego.

Park Regulations

Anza-Borrego Desert State Park has no entrance fee. It is also one of the few California parks that permit open camping. The open-camping policy has resulted in a tradition of care and consideration; roadside campsites are clean and well cared for. Vehicles must remain within one car-length of the road, and all fires must be enclosed in metal containers. Visitors should not camp within 200 yards of water sources to protect animals' access to water. Developed fee campgrounds are near the visitor center in Borrego Springs and at Tamarisk Grove; open camping is not permitted near these two sites. Several undeveloped no-fee campgrounds are also located throughout the park.

All vehicles must be highway legal and must stay on the 500 miles of established roads within the park. Drivers must be licensed. Ocotillo Wells State Vehicular Recreation Area is immediately east of the park on CA 78 for off-road-vehicle driving, where a driver's license is not required

In Anza-Borrego, bicycles too must remain on the paved and dirt roads. There are more than 500 miles of roads in the park open to bicycles. The park has published a new mountain-biking guide, available at any ranger station.

No dogs are permitted on the trails of Anza-Borrego. On roadways and in campgrounds, dogs must be on leashes no longer than 6 feet. It is advised that you leave your pet at home. Lack of water, heat, coyotes, cacti, and rattlesnakes all make the desert inhospitable to pets.

Backcountry permits are not required for backpacking. However, registering your trip plan with the ranger at the regional ranger station is recommended for safety.

All cultural and natural contents of the park are protected by state law. No collecting of any kind is permitted. Carrying a loaded weapon of any kind and hunting are likewise forbidden in the park.

The visitor center just west of Borrego Springs is open daily 9:00 A.M. to 5:00 P.M. from October through May. From June through September it is open only on weekends and holidays from 9:00 A.M. to 5:00 P.M. Maps, publications, slide and video shows, and informational exhibits are available here. There is also a signed nature trail featuring much of the variety of desert plants found in the Colorado (Sonoran) Desert. Check here for current regulations and road conditions. Several self-guided-hike brochures are available at the visitor center, providing information for hikes and auto tours throughout the park.

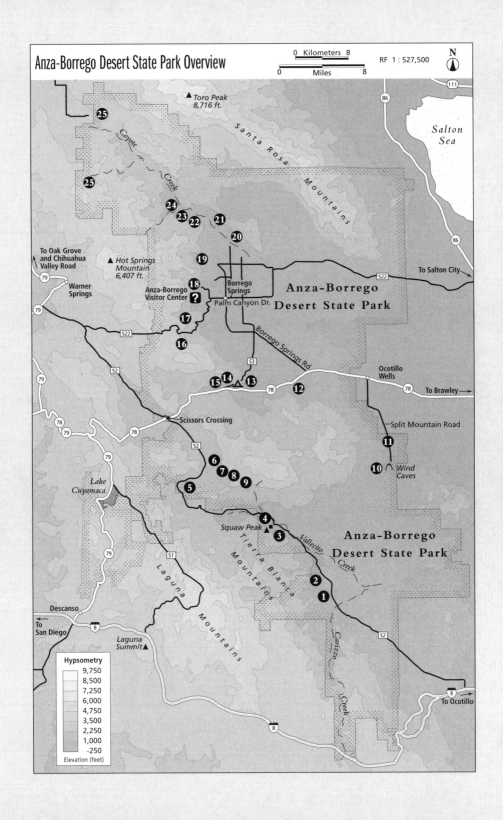

Anza-Borrego Desert State Park Overview

0 Kilometers 8

0 Miles 8

RF 1 : 527,500

N

▲ Toro Peak 8,716 ft.

Salton Sea

Santa Rosa Mountains

Coyote Creek

25

25

24

23 22 21

20

19

▲ Hot Springs Mountain 6,407 ft.

18

Borrego Springs

Anza-Borrego Visitor Center

?

17

16

Palm Canyon Dr.

Anza-Borrego Desert State Park

To Oak Grove and Chihuahua Valley Road

Warner Springs

To Salton City

S22

Borrego Springs Rd

S3

Ocotillo Wells

To Brawley

15 14 △ 13

78

12

S22

79

S2

79

78

79

Scissors Crossing

S2

79

Lake Cuyamaca

Split Mountain Road

11

10 ⌒ Wind Caves

6

7 8 9

5

4

Squaw Peak ▲ 3

Vallecito Creek

Anza-Borrego Desert State Park

79

S1

Tierra Blanca Mountains

2

1

Laguna Mountains

Descanso

To San Diego

8

Laguna Summit ▲

Carrizo Creek

S2

8

To Ocotillo

8

Hypsometry

9,750
8,500
7,250
6,000
4,750
3,500
2,250
1,000
-250

Elevation (feet)

Anza-Borrego Desert State Park Hikes at a Glance

Hike (Number)	Distance	Difficulty*	Features	Page
Alcoholic Pass (20)	3.4 miles	M	vista	63
Borrego Palm Canyon Nature Trail (19)	3.5 miles	M	oasis	61
Box Canyon Overlook (5)	1.8 miles	E	historic site	30
Cactus Loop Trail (14)	1.0 mile	E	nature trail	50
California R & H Trail (17)	8.5 miles	S	vistas	55
Cougar Canyon (23)	3.0 miles	M/S	canyon	71
Elephant Trees Nature Trail (11)	1.0 mile	E	nature trail	44
Foot and Walker Pass (6)	0.2 mile	E	historic site	33
Ghost Mountain (7)	2.0 miles	M	historic site, vista	34
Indian Canyon (22)	4.5 miles	S	canyon	69
Kenyon Overlook Trail Loop (13)	1.0 mile	E	vista	47
Lower Willows (21)	4.0 miles	M	stream, canyon	66
Moonlight Canyon (3)	1.5 miles	M	canyon	25
The Morteros (8)	0.5 mile	E	archaeological site	37
Mountain Palm Springs Loop (1)	6.5 miles	M	oases	19
Narrows Earth Trail (12)	0.5 mile	E	geology	46
Pacific Crest Trail S. (25)	5.0 miles	S	mountain peak	77
Pacific Crest Trail N. (25)	5.0 miles	M	mountain peak	77
Panorama Overlook/Extended Overlook (18)	2.6 miles	S	vista	58
Pictograph Trail (9)	3.0 miles	E	archaeological site	39
Sheep Canyon (24)	3.0 miles	S	canyon, oasis	74
Squaw Peak/Pond (4)	1.9 miles	E	vista, oasis	28
Torote Canyon (2)	4.0 miles	M	elephant trees	23
Wilson Trail (16)	11.0 miles	M	vistas	52
Wind Caves (10)	1.4 miles	M	geology, archaeological site	41
Yaqui Well Nature Trail (15)	2.0 miles	E	nature trail	51

*E=easy, M=moderate, S=strenuous

1 Mountain Palm Springs Loop

This loop trail in the eastern Tierra Blanca Mountains has several short but steep climbs as it leads to two short forks. Here you will find several native palm groves at isolated oases. These hidden patches of greenery provide excellent birding sites.

Start: About 52 miles south of Borrego Springs.
Distance: 6.5-mile loop with two side trips.
Approximate hiking time: 5 hours.
Difficulty: Moderate.
Trail surface: Mostly clear trail with several clear wash stretches along with short, good sections of rocky cutoff trails.

Seasons: October through April.
USGS topo map: Sweeney Pass-CA (1:24,000).
Trail contact: Anza-Borrego Desert State Park (see appendix D).

Finding the trailhead: From the park visitor center, go 1.9 miles east on Palm Canyon Drive to Christmas Circle; from the circle, take Borrego Springs Road (S3) south for 5.6 miles to the Y intersection, where you bear right. Continue on S3 7.4 miles to the Tamarisk Grove intersection with California Highway 78. Go right (west) on CA 78 for 7.4 miles to Scissors Crossing. Turn left (south) on Park Route S2. Drive 31.8 miles south on S2. Shortly after mile marker 47, turn right (west) onto the dirt road for the Mountain Palm Springs Campground. Continue 0.5 mile to the trailhead and parking area.

The Hike

The Mountain Palm Springs oasis loop is really two separate hikes from the same trailhead to the end point of both hikes: the extensive Palm Bowl Grove. The resulting combination is a wonderful loop to all six of the captivating palm groves in the Mountain Palm Springs complex. Both trails lead up sandy washes, one westward and the other to the north. It is preferable to begin on the south leg of the loop by heading west to the Pygmy Grove, but it makes little difference which way you hike the loop.

The native California fan palm derives its name from the shape of its leaves. As the tree produces new leaves at the top of its trunk, skirts of older leaves die and droop over the lower part of the tree, giving it the distinctive full look characteristic of these palms. These groves are remnants of ancient savannahs. Here water and shade attract scores of bird species, such as the hooded oriole, which weaves its nest on the underside of palm fronds. You may also catch a glimpse of a great horned owl, mourning dove, cactus wren, or western bluebird. In the fall coyotes help regenerate the trees by eating their tiny fruits and leaving seed-laden droppings in new locations.

On the south end of the loop, head west up a sandy wash to the first small grove of four large palm trees at 0.4 mile. Continue up the main wash another 0.4 mile to Pygmy Grove, named after the larger grove of short, fire-scarred trees. The third

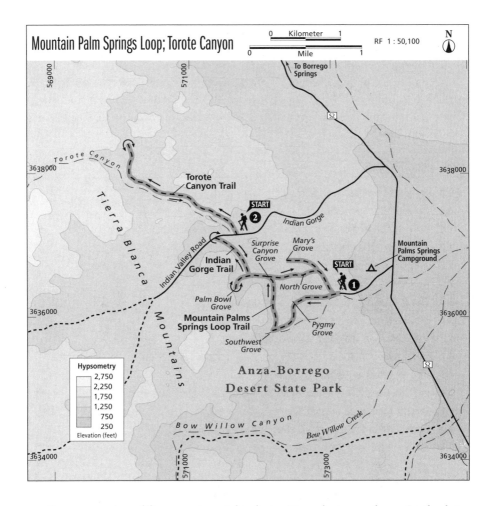

0   Kilometer   1

0   Mile   1

RF 1 : 50,100

N

To Borrego
Springs

S2

Torote Canyon

3638000

3638000

Torote
Canyon Trail

Tierra Blanca

START

2

Indian Gorge

Surprise
Canyon
Grove

Mary's
Grove

Mountain
Palms Springs
Campground

Indian Valley Road

Indian
Gorge Trail

START

1

North Grove

Palm Bowl
Grove

3636000

3636000

Mountains

Mountain Palms
Springs Loop Trail

Pygmy
Grove

Southwest
Grove

Anza-Borrego
Desert State Park

S2

Hypsometry

2,750
2,250
1,750
1,250
750
250
Elevation (feet)

Bow Willow Canyon

Bow Willow Creek

3634000

571000

573000

3634000

569000

571000

small grove consists of five trees in a tight cluster. From here a rocky ravine leads to the right another 0.2 mile to a single palm tree. Turn left up the main valley to a fork in the trail at 1.2 miles. Continue to the right another 0.3 mile to the sizable Southwest Grove, which can be seen straight ahead. Pools of water and nearby elephant trees make this peaceful oasis an enjoyable interlude during the loop hike.

From Southwest Grove, take a fairly distinct trail northward over a rocky ridge 1 mile to Surprise Canyon. From here turn left and walk up the canyon another 0.5 mile to the largest and most luxuriant grove in the complex, Palm Bowl. On the way back down from Palm Bowl Grove, look for the signed Indian Gorge Cutoff Trail leading to the north. This old Indian trail is signed 0.5 MILE TO INDIAN GORGE. The actual distance is closer to 0.7 mile. The narrow, rocky trail gains 200 feet to the top

◀ *The palms of Mary's Grove are tightly clustered on the north end of the Mountain Palm Springs Loop.*

of the ridge then angles down left into Indian Valley. The round-trip distance from Surprise Canyon to Indian Valley is 1.4 miles, providing yet more variety to this already diverse hiking loop.

To complete the loop from Surprise Canyon, continue down the wash to the parking area/trailhead. North Grove is reached 0.5 mile down the canyon, Mary's Grove is a 0.6-mile side trip to the left, and from this junction the trailhead is only another 0.5 mile.

Miles and Directions

0.0   From the trailhead, head west up the sandy wash.

0.8   Arrive at Pygmy Grove.

1.0   Turn left next to a single palm tree and head up the main wash.

1.2   Stay right at the fork in the trail.

1.5   Arrive at Southwest Grove.

2.5   At Surprise Canyon, turn left and walk up to Palm Bowl Grove.

3.0   This is Palm Bowl Grove, the turnaround point.

3.3   Turn left (north) on the signed Indian Gorge Trail.

4.0   Use the turnaround point at Indian Valley Road.

4.7   You're back at Surprise Canyon for completion of the 1.4-mile out-and-back side hike.

4.9   Turn left (east) at Surprise Canyon Grove.

5.4   At North Grove, turn left (north) for the short walk to Mary's Grove.

5.7   Use the turnaround point at Mary's Grove.

6.0   Back at North Grove, continue south to the trailhead.

6.5   Complete the loop back at the trailhead.

Option: If you start the hike on the northern leg of the loop, the trail leads north from the parking area up a sandy wash or, if you prefer firmer footing, up the right bank of the wash. Straight ahead you can catch a glimpse of palm trees 0.2 mile farther. The wash grows progressively rockier as you approach Mary's Grove, where huge 30- to 40-foot palms tower above the rocky gorge. Retrace your steps 0.3 mile back down the wash to the trailpost that marks the mouth of the wash that runs westward. The intersection is rocky, but this new wash becomes sandy as it gains slightly in elevation.

As you continue west up the new wash, you will pass North Grove, which consists of several clumps of palm trees, providing a delightful shady interlude in your journey. One spot to keep in mind for later is a distinctive row of palms (appropriately called Surprise Canyon Grove), for it is there that a marked cutoff trail climbs over the ridge to the south to the Southwest Grove. Meanwhile, however, keep moving west, because another lovely surprise awaits you: a huge array of majestic palms arranged like an orchestra in an amphitheater valley. This is the Palm Bowl Grove. Plan on allowing ample time to enjoy this magical place before hiking back down the wash.

2 Torote Canyon

Torote Canyon is a half-day out-and-back hike through a sandy wash and boulder-strewn canyon with intermittent wide basins ringed by rugged rock ridges. A sizable "herd" of elephant trees can be seen within the first 0.5 mile.

See map on page 21.
Start: About 50 miles south of Borrego Springs.
Distance: 4 miles out and back.
Approximate hiking time: 2 hours.
Difficulty: Moderate.
Trail surface: A use trail follows the main wash with easy routes over and around boulders.

Seasons: October through April.
USGS topo maps: Aqua Caliente Springs-CA; Arroyo Tapiado-CA; Sombrero Peak-CA; and Sweeney Pass-CA (1:24,000).
Trail contact: Anza-Borrego Desert State Park (see appendix D).

Finding the trailhead: From the park visitor center, drive east 1.9 miles to Christmas Circle, turn right on Borrego Springs Road (S3), and drive south for 5.6 miles to the Y intersection; turn right (south) on S3 and drive 7.4 miles to the junction with California Highway 78. Turn right on CA 78 and drive another 7.4 miles to Scissors Crossing. Turn left (south) on Park Route S2 and drive 29.6 miles to the signed Indian Valley Road. Turn right (southwest) and drive 1.8 miles up the sandy road to the mouth of Torote Canyon, which is marked with a small sign. A monument called "El Torote" faces away from the road into the canyon. Park and begin the hike here.

The Hike

Hike up the sandy-wash use trail of Torote Canyon, which, for the most part, makes a good and easy-to-follow trail. At times you will need to scramble up and over an occasional boulder-clogged segment of the wash, but in general the going is easy enough to allow enjoyment of the remote surroundings of the canyon. You'll come to the first elephant tree on the left slope (south side) in less than 0.4 mile, but keep going for a good look at a dense "herd" of elephant trees.

The Spanish word *torote* means "twisted," referring to the gnarled growth pattern of the elephant trees, which are widespread in Mexico. At about 0.6 mile (1,180 feet), a large group of trees clings to the steep, rocky slopes above the canyon floor. Take time to get better acquainted with Borrego's rarest tree: Feel its parchmentlike bark, take note of its small, feathery leaves, and breathe deeply of its pleasant cedarlike aroma. At about 0.9 mile the canyon opens up into the first wide valley, which stretches a good 0.5 mile to the northwest. At the head of the valley, the main Torote Canyon continues up a bouldery draw to the northwest. Instead of continuing up the main canyon, follow what appears to be the main valley northward to the right. This leads to a short, tight canyon that opens after about 300 yards to the second wide valley. Continue up the valley to a low pass straight ahead.

Elephant trees in Torote Canyon.

Although several cross-country routes are possible—eastward to Carrizo Valley or to the south toward the north fork of Indian Valley—the upper end of this second wide valley is a good turnaround point for this pleasant 4-mile round-trip journey. But go back only after you've given yourself enough time to savor the remote upper canyon's magic.

Miles and Directions

0.0 Start at the trailhead at the mouth of Torote Canyon (1,060 feet).

0.6 Arrive at a sizable "herd" of elephant trees.

1.0 This is the first wide basin you'll come to.

1.5 With the main Torote Canyon to the left, turn right (north) at the canyon junction.

2.0 At the turnaround point at a low pass above a second wide valley (1,600 feet), return to the trailhead by the same route.

4.0 Arrive back at the trailhead.

3 Moonlight Canyon

Moonlight Canyon is a colorful gem of a canyon within the state park, although its trailhead lies within Agua Caliente County Park.

Start: About 43 miles south of Borrego Springs, in Agua Caliente County Park.
Distance: 1.5-mile loop.
Approximate hiking time: 1 hour.
Difficulty: Moderate.
Trail surface: Clear sandy trail, clear wash.

Seasons: October through April.
USGS topo map: Agua Caliente Springs-CA (1:24,000).
Trail contact: Agua Caliente County Park and Anza-Borrego Desert State Park (see appendix D).

Finding the trailhead: From the park visitor center, drive east on Palm Canyon Drive 1.9 miles to Christmas Circle. Turn south at the circle on S3 (Borrego Springs Road) 5.6 miles to the Y intersection. Bear right and continue south on S3 for 7.4 miles to its intersection with California Highway 78 just beyond the Tamarisk Grove Campground. Turn right (west) on CA 78 and go 7.4 miles to Scissors Crossing. At the crossing turn left (south) on S2 and drive 22.3 miles to the turnoff to Agua Caliente Springs and Campground. Turn right and continue 0.5 mile to the trailhead at the parking area adjacent to the park gate. There is a daily park entrance fee; check with the county park, as the fee increases annually. The trailhead leaves from campsites no. 39 and 40 and returns near campsite no. 63.

The Hike

Although the trailhead lies outside of the Anza–Borrego boundary and there is an entry fee to the county park, it is definitely worth a visit. Interesting erosion formations, intermittent watery spots, and cozy side canyons combine for a series of discoveries as you follow the well-marked trail through its circular route in the canyon.

The trail begins inauspiciously by climbing to a low ridge; it quickly drops to the stream bottom, which goes up a rocky draw and into the canyon itself. Side washes and small canyons periodically invite further exploration as the main wash winds downward. There are occasional steep slopes requiring only simple scrambling on this otherwise easy hike. The rock formations, courtesy of centuries of water and earthquake activity, are endlessly fascinating. The variety of colors of the rocks is also noteworthy. Where water exists, sudden splashes of greenery—tamarisk and willow patches—punctuate the trip.

The canyon empties into a wide dry wash, leading to a rock-lined trail that winds through an ocotillo forest and back to the campground at site no. 63, down the hill from your starting point.

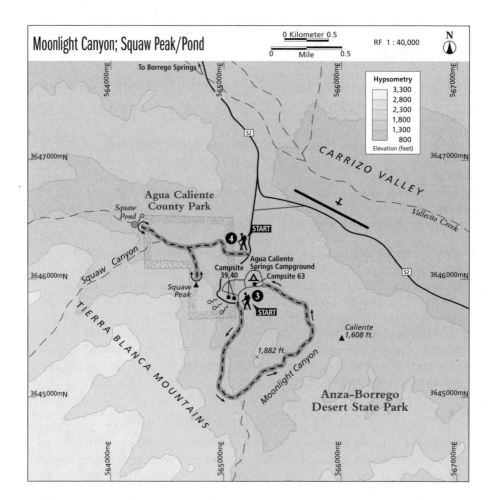

Miles and Directions

0.0 The trailhead is located at campsites no. 39 and 40.

1.0 The trail enters the main wash.

1.1 At the signposted junction, the short box canyon is a worthy side trip.

1.3 You'll see an open ocotillo forest as the canyon broadens.

1.5 End the hike near campsite no. 63.

Dropping into the narrow of Moonlight Canyon. ▶

4 Squaw Peak/Pond

This is a short climb on the edge of the Tierra Blanca Mountains to a scenic overlook of the Carrizo Valley and Vallecito Mountains, combined with a sandy-wash hike to a favored watering hole for wildlife.

See map on page 26.
Start: About 43 miles south of Borrego Springs, in Agua Caliente County Park.
Distance: 1.9 miles out and back.
Approximate hiking time: Between 1 and 2 hours.
Difficulty: Easy.

Trail surface: Clear sandy trail.
Seasons: November through April.
USGS topo map: Agua Caliente Springs-CA (1:24,000).
Trail contact: Agua Caliente Springs Regional County Park (see appendix D).

Finding the trailhead: From the Anza-Borrego visitor center, head east on Palm Canyon Drive for 1.9 miles to Christmas Circle. Turn south at the circle on S3 (Borrego Springs Road) 5.6 miles to the Y intersection; bear right at the Y and continue south on S3 for 7.4 miles to its intersection with California Highway 78 just beyond the Tamarisk Grove Campground. Turn right (west) on CA 78 and go 7.4 miles to Scissors Crossing. At the crossing turn left (south) on S2 and drive 22.3 miles to the turnoff to Agua Caliente Springs. Turn right and drive 0.5 mile to the trailhead at the parking area adjacent to the park entrance. There is a park entrance fee, which changes annually; contact the park for details. The trailhead is directly north of the ranger station. Cross the parking lot to a low ridge on the right next to the campfire circle and take the path that leads to the campground amphitheater and the Squaw Peak/Pond trailhead.

The Hike

From the Agua Caliente Springs parking area, pick up the Squaw Peak/Pond trail near the campfire circle just above the ranger station/park entrance. Climb 0.1 mile to the ridgetop trail junction. Take the left trail 0.25 mile to 1,450-foot Squaw Peak. From the junction, the trail makes switchbacks up 150 feet to this overlook of the Carrizo Valley and Badlands and the more distant Vallecito Mountains.

To reach Squaw Pond, drop back to the junction and continue left down to the sandy Squaw Canyon wash. Turn left up the well-traveled wash past clumps of honey mesquite, an important food staple for early-day Cahuilla Indians. Mesquite are adorned with cylindrical spikes of yellow flowers in late spring.

Squaw Pond is 0.5 mile up the wash. Tracks of coyote, bobcat, and a host of smaller animals tell the tale of their visitation to this desert spring oasis shaded by dense willow and a single palm tree. Bring your binoculars for excellent bird watching at Squaw Pond. The surrounding hillsides are dotted with barrel and cholla cactus.

After savoring this tranquil setting, the most direct return to the trailhead is to simply walk all the way back down the wash, which intersects the road just below

The Anza-Borrego Desert stretches to the north from Squaw Peak.

the parking area. In so doing, you'll avoid the additional climb back over the ridge to the trail junction.

After the hike you might enjoy a soak in the mineral hot springs of Agua Caliente. A shallow outdoor pool averages around ninety-five degrees and is open during the day. A larger indoor Jacuzzi pool is kept slightly warmer. The natural hot-water source is an offshoot of the Elsinore Fault.

Miles and Directions

0.0 Start at the trailhead.

0.1 At the trail junction, turn left to the Squaw Peak overlook.

0.35 Arrive at the Squaw Peak overlook (1,450 feet).

0.6 Return to the trail junction (1,290 feet) and turn left toward the pond.

0.7 Arrive at the Squaw Canyon wash (1,240 feet).

1.2 Use the turnaround point at Squaw Pond (1,280 feet).

1.9 Arrive back at the parking area trailhead.

5 Box Canyon Overlook

This historic mountain pass on the Old Southern Emigrant Trail was used by forty-niners and other emigrants, as well as the Butterfield Overland Stage. You can simply view it from the overlook or take a winding path down to the trail itself to get a real feel for the challenges that faced the early pioneers.

Start: About 31 miles south of Borrego Springs.
Distance: 1.8 miles out and back.
Approximate hiking time: Up to 2 hours.
Difficulty: Easy.
Trail surface: Clear trail, clear wash.

Seasons: October through April.
USGS topo map: Earthquake Valley-CA (1:24,000).
Trail contact: Anza-Borrego Desert State Park (see appendix D).

Box Canyon wash.

Box Canyon Overlook; Foot and Walker Pass

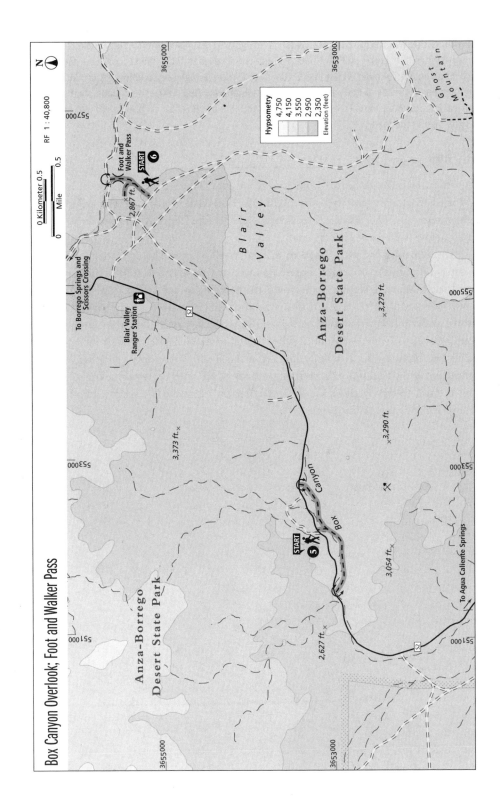

Finding the trailhead: From the visitor center, go east 1.9 miles to Christmas Circle in Borrego Springs; turn south on Park Route S3 and go 5.6 miles to the Y intersection. Bear right and continue on S3 7.4 miles to the intersection with California Highway 78. Turn right on CA 78 and go another 7.4 miles to Scissors Crossing. Turn left on Park Route S2 and continue south 9 miles. About 0.6 mile south of mile marker 25 on S2 is the Box Canyon parking pullout on the south side of the road.

The Hike

Much Anza–Borrego history coincides at this spot! The Southern Emigrant Trail, the Mormon Battalion, and the Butterfield Overland Mail Route used this arduous low mountain pass. The historical marker is right by the highway; the overlook of the trail below is 250 feet farther south.

By following the path down to the trail itself, you quickly get a feeling for the obstacle that this rocky ridge represented for early travelers. To follow a piece of the trail itself, hike the sloping path down to the right to a wooden post marked U.S. MORMON BATTALION TRAIL. At this point the trail coincides with the wash. The historic wash trail is marked with an occasional wooden post. Follow the gently graded wash down 0.7 mile to a pullout where S2 almost touches the wash. Your hike parallels the highway but is wholly hidden in the small canyon to provide a feeling of seclusion and communion with the hundreds of previous users of this trail segment.

Return to the overlook via the wash, not the highway. The narrow blind curves make it dangerous at this point.

6 Foot and Walker Pass

A short hike to an overlook at Blair Valley provides you with a view of the Butter-field Overland Stage's route over Puerta Pass. Here you may gain sympathy for both horses and passengers as they made their way through this rocky landscape.

See map on page 31.
Start: About 31 miles south of Borrego Springs.
Distance: 0.2 mile out and back.
Approximate hiking time: 30 minutes.
Difficulty: Easy.

Trail surface: Clear sandy and rocky trail.
Seasons: October through April.
USGS topo map: Earthquake Valley-CA (1:24,000).
Trail contact: Anza-Borrego Desert State Park (see appendix D).

The California Riding and Hiking Trail extends northward.

Finding the trailhead: From the park visitor center, go east 1.9 miles to Christmas Circle; turn south on Borrego Springs Road (S3) and go 5.6 miles to the Y intersection. Bear right and continue on S3 7.4 miles to the intersection with California Highway 78. Turn right on CA 78 and go another 7.4 miles to Scissors Crossing. Turn left on S2 and go 6.3 miles to the Blair Valley turnoff, on your left. The Foot and Walker Trail historical monument is 0.3 mile from the turnoff on the north side of the valley.

The Hike

This short trail provides an excellent orientation to the Blair Valley region, with its layers of human use, from prehistoric (pictographs and morteros) to historic (routes through Box Canyon and Foot and Walker Pass) to recent (the South home on Ghost Mountain) times.

Here at the entrance to the valley, the Butterfield Stage had difficulty with the pass, especially if the coach had a heavy load. Often passengers had to hop out and walk—hence the name of the pass.

From the pullout on the dirt road below the hill above you, a use trail goes up the rise to a historic marker. A second use trail goes through the pass itself. A brief hike in this area reminds us of the arduous conditions for nineteenth-century desert travelers.

7 Ghost Mountain: Marshal South Home

The steep rugged trail to the remains of a primitive adobe home built in 1932 on top of isolated Ghost Mountain rewards you with a spectacular view.

Start: About 31 miles south of Borrego Springs.
Distance: 2 miles out and back.
Approximate hiking time: 2 hours allows you to explore the homesite.
Difficulty: Moderate.

Trail surface: Clear but rocky trail up the mountain, with some constructed stone steps in steep places.
Seasons: October through April.
USGS topo map: Earthquake Valley-CA (1:24,000).
Trail contact: Anza-Borrego Desert State Park (see appendix D).

Finding the trailhead: From the visitor center, drive east 1.9 miles to Christmas Circle in Borrego Springs. Turn south on Park Route S3, then drive 5.6 miles to the Y intersection; bear right at the Y and continue on S3 7.4 miles to the intersection with California Highway 78. Turn right on CA 78 and go another 7.4 miles to the intersection with Park Route S2 at Scissors Crossing. Turn south (left) on S2. Blair Valley is 6.3 miles southeast of Scissors Crossing, on your left at mile 23. Turn left onto the dirt road. The road junctions in Blair Valley are clearly marked with signs. Go straight on the dirt road and turn right at the T intersection for the Ghost Mountain parking area, 3.2 miles from S2.

The stone remnants of the Marshal South home on Ghost Mountain.

The Hike

Poet Marshal South was an early refugee from civilization, fleeing with his family in the 1930s to this remote desert mountaintop, named Yaquitepec. This hike is an interesting mixture of scenic splendor and devastating squalor—the South home was primitive at best. The remains of the family's attempt to live atop a mountain peak in this valley create a striking contrast with the awesome views in every direction. No water is available; remains of a cistern system sit on the boulders near the cooking area. Fuel is also nonexistent. Living here was hard work.

The path snakes its way to the mountaintop with a series of steps and switchbacks. Marshal South built quite a trail; there are even steps on some of the steeper stretches. It is thought provoking to imagine what it would be like to transport essentials up this hillside and rear three children in such a location. When you arrive at the house site, the ruins reveal how basic life was for the South family. This was no castle. Of course, the dwelling has fallen into severe disrepair.

Ghost Mountain: Marshal South Home; The Morteros; Pictograph Trail

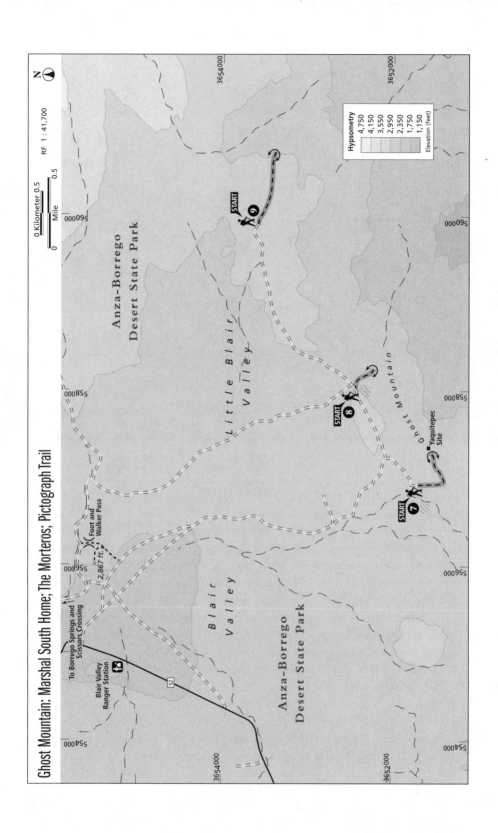

Since both sunrise and sunset are spectacular from Ghost Mountain, campers have used the two or three sites available here, apparently with no trouble from the ghost. However, to protect the homesite, the park does not encourage camping there. The South family surely enjoyed the view. Many interesting tales exist among local residents about the family and its escapades. According to one source, Marshal South eventually left his family and the mountain, going to live with a lady librarian in a nearby town.

8 The Morteros

An easy path leads to the site of a Native American settlement with ancient grinding holes cut into granitic boulders.

Several morteros were ground into this large flat rock at the end of the Morteros Trail.

See map on page 36.
Start: About 31 miles south of Borrego Springs.
Distance: 0.5 mile out and back.
Approximate hiking time: 30 minutes.
Difficulty: Easy.

Trail surface: Broad, clear dirt trail.
Seasons: October through April.
USGS topo maps: Earthquake Valley-CA (1:24,000) and Whale Peak-CA (1:24,000).
Trail contact: Anza-Borrego Desert State Park (see appendix D).

Finding the trailhead: From the visitor center, drive east on Palm Canyon Drive 1.9 miles to Christmas Circle. Turn south on Park Route S3. At 5.6 miles south of the circle, bear right at the Y intersection and continue 7.4 miles on S3 to the intersection with California Highway 78. Turn right on CA 78 and go 7.4 miles to Scissors Crossing. Turn left on S2 and go south 6.3 miles. At mile marker 23 is the Blair Valley road. Turn left onto the dirt road. At the stop sign at the first intersection in Blair Valley, a park sign indicates distances and directions to three trails. Follow the dirt road and turn left to the Morteros pullout, 3.7 miles from the stop sign.

The Hike

A broad, sandy trail leads from the parking lot up the rise to the site of a prehistoric village set against the rock-strewn hillside. The slight elevation gain provides a sweeping view of Little Blair Valley, stretching to the northwest. Huge obelisk-like boulders frame large horizontal granite stones, in which the *morteros,* or mortar stones, were worn over a thousand years of grinding by the Kumeyaay Indians. Fortunately the site has been respected by visitors and remains in the same condition as when the Indians departed, giving it a hallowed feeling.

9 Pictograph Trail

This short hike leads to a major pictograph site and an overlook of Vallecito Valley.

See map on page 36.
Start: About 31 miles south of Borrego Springs.
Distance: 3 miles out and back.
Approximate hiking time: 1 to 2 hours.
Difficulty: Easy.

Trail surface: Broad dirt path.
Seasons: October through April.
USGS topo map: Whale Peak-CA (1:24,000).
Trail contact: Anza-Borrego Desert State Park (see appendix D).

Finding the trailhead: From the visitor center, drive east on Palm Canyon Drive 1.9 miles to Christmas Circle. Turn south on Park Route S3. At 5.6 miles south of the circle, bear right at the Y intersection and continue 7.4 miles on S3 to the intersection with California Highway 78. Turn

Pictographs are found at mile 1 along the Pictograph Trail.

right on CA 78 and go 7.4 miles to Scissors Crossing. Turn left on S2 and go south 6.3 miles. At mile marker 23 is the Blair Valley road. Turn left (southeast) on the Blair Valley road. Follow this dirt road, turning left at the T intersection, 5 miles to the Pictograph Trail parking area/trailhead.

The Hike

Blair Valley has attracted human visitors for centuries. High above the desert, its temperatures are more moderate than those of its surroundings. Early inhabitants evidently found it comfortable, as do present-day hikers and campers.

A wide, sandy trail leads from the parking lot up a gradual slope to a saddle 160 feet higher than the parking area. The trail becomes more rocky as it climbs through piñon-juniper vegetation. Over the saddle, at 0.4 mile on your right, is a large boulder with the mysterious pictographs (identified as petroglyphs on the topographic map) left by prehistoric residents of this high valley. These striking artifacts of an ancient culture have been well preserved despite their remote, wild location. Hikers can pause to contemplate the meaning of these signs, which still puzzle archaeologists.

About 0.5 mile farther down the sandy-wash path is a sharply defined notch in a rocky ridge; through the notch is the overlook of Vallecitos Valley and the Vallecitos Mountains. Whale Peak (5,349 feet) is prominent to the northeast. There's an abrupt 100-foot precipice at the overlook, so keep an eye on overly adventurous members of your hiking party.

Your view of Little Blair Valley on the hike back to the parking area shows the value of this location to early desert dwellers. Residents enjoyed excellent visibility from this slope at the end of the valley. There's a sacred feeling about being in an area that was lived in so many centuries ago.

10 Wind Caves

Although it involves a long drive, this short hike features an interesting geologic and archaeological site located on a ridgetop, with a sweeping view of the Carrizo Badlands.

Start: About 38 miles southeast of Borrego Springs.
Distance: 1.4-mile out and back (add 0.5 mile for exploring the caves).
Approximate hiking time: 1 to 2 hours.
Difficulty: Moderate.

Trail surface: Dirt trail.
Seasons: October through April.
USGS topo map: Carrizo Mountain NE-CA (1:24,000).
Trail contact: Anza-Borrego Desert State Park (see appendix D).

Finding the trailhead: From the park visitor center in Borrego Springs, take Palm Canyon Drive 1.9 miles east to Christmas Circle; at the circle, turn south on Borrego Springs Road. In 5.6 miles, at the intersection with Park Route S3, continue straight on Borrego Springs Road 6.6 miles to the intersection with California Highway 78. Turn left on CA 78; go 6.7 miles east to Ocotillo Wells. At the main intersection in town, turn right (south) onto Split Mountain Road. Continue past Elephant Trees to the right turn onto Split Mountain or Fish Creek Wash at 10.8 miles. Drive up the sandy wash 5.1 miles to a small Wind Caves sign indicating the trail on your left. The trailhead is just south of the narrows of Split Mountain wash. The wash is not difficult for a passenger vehicle, but it should definitely be avoided in wet or threatening weather. This road often requires four-wheel drive. Check conditions at the visitor center before taking this road.

The Hike

The trip's excitement begins with the drive up the wash. Progressing upward from the valley floor, the wash approaches the rocky face of Split Mountain—then cuts through the mountain, with hardly any gain in elevation. The trailhead is beyond this narrow spot in the wash.

The first 0.2 mile of trail climbs from the floor of the wash to the ridge via a rocky but well-defined trail. The view of the Carrizo Badlands behind you is spectacular. A variety of worn footpaths lead from the edge of the wash into the lands above; some of these routes are believed to be remnants of prehistoric use of the area. They all converge on the caves, so it does not matter which one you choose.

Around 0.6 mile the caves come into view. A lower, smaller set of these fascinating sandstone wind-sculpted formations lies slightly below the larger set. There is an extraterrestrial quality about the site, due to both its ethereal appearance and the evidence that early Indians made use of these natural shelters. You may walk another 0.5 mile while exploring the caves. On your return trip down Split Mountain wash, watch for additional wind-cave formations high above the rim on the right.

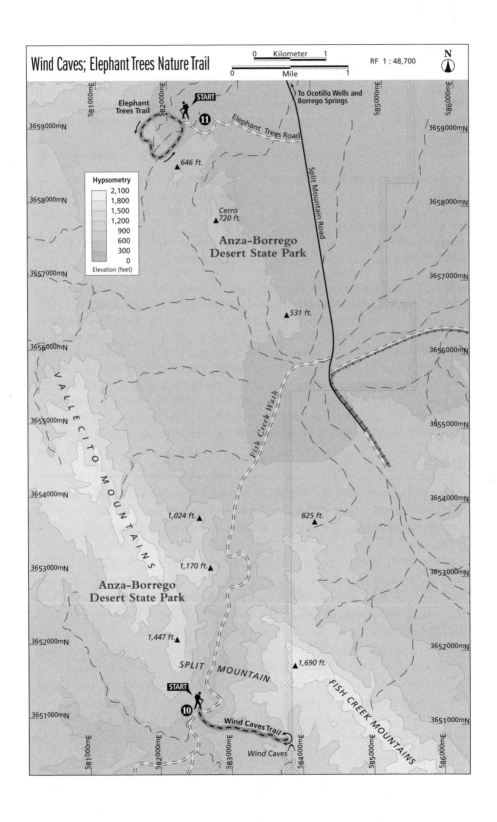

Wind Caves; Elephant Trees Nature Trail

Elephant Trees Trail

START

11

Elephant Trees Road

To Ocotillo Wells and Borrego Springs

646 ft.

Split Mountain Road

Cerro
720 ft.

Anza-Borrego Desert State Park

531 ft.

Fish Creek Wash

VALLECITO MOUNTAINS

1,024 ft.

825 ft.

1,170 ft.

Anza-Borrego Desert State Park

1,447 ft.

1,690 ft.

SPLIT MOUNTAIN

START

10

Wind Caves Trail

Wind Caves

FISH CREEK MOUNTAINS

Hypsometry

| 2,100 |
| 1,800 |
| 1,500 |
| 1,200 |
| 900 |
| 600 |
| 300 |
| 0 |

Elevation (feet)

0 Kilometer 1

0 Mile 1

RF 1 : 48,700

N

581000mE
582000mE
585000mE
586000mE
581000mE
582000mE
583000mE
584000mE
585000mE
586000mE

3659000mN
3658000mN
3657000mN
3656000mN
3655000mN
3654000mN
3653000mN
3652000mN
3651000mN

The wind-eroded sandstone of Wind Caves forms an unearthly appearance high on the ridge above Split Mountain wash.

Miles and Directions

0.0 The trail climbs steeply from the wash to the plateau above.

0.3 Take any one of the variety of trails here, all of which head easterly.

0.7 Arrive at Wind Caves and the turnaround point (after exploring caves).

1.4 Return to the trailhead (add 0.5 mile for exploring the caves).

11 Elephant Trees Nature Trail

This easy self-guided loop displays the diverse plant community of an alluvial fan and desert wash. The name is deceiving since there remains only one of the rare and unusual elephant trees.

See map on page 42.
Start: About 32 miles southeast of Borrego Springs.
Distance: 1-mile loop.
Approximate hiking time: 1 hour.
Difficulty: Easy.

Trail surface: Broad dirt trail.
Seasons: October through April.
USGS topo map: Borrego Mountain SE-CA (1:24,000).
Trail contact: Anza-Borrego Desert State Park (see appendix D).

Elephant trees—Anza-Borrego's most unusual plant.

Finding the trailhead: From the park visitor center in Borrego Springs, go east 1.9 miles on Palm Canyon Drive to Christmas Circle. Take Borrego Springs Road south from the circle for 5.6 miles to Park Route S3. At the intersection with S3, go straight (southeast) on Borrego Springs Road toward Ocotillo Wells. Borrego Springs Road meets California Highway 78 in 6.6 miles. Go left (east) on CA 78 for 6.7 miles to Ocotillo Wells. Turn right (south) at the Ocotillo Wells intersection onto Split Mountain Road and drive 5.9 miles to Elephant Trees Road. Turn right (west) and follow the dirt road 1 mile to the parking area/trailhead.

The Hike

This well-signed self-guided nature trail climbs gently up a rock-lined wash to a solitary elephant tree. An informative brochure is available at the trailhead.

The unusual elephant tree of the Sonoran Desert was not discovered and identified by botanists until 1937. There used to be a herd of elephants, and now one rogue elephant remains. This example of the species was long thought to be the northernmost group of elephant trees in California. However, in 1987 another grove of almost 200 elephant trees was discovered on the western slopes of the Santa Rosa Mountains, 21 miles farther north. Numbering only in the hundreds, they cling precariously to boulders and steep side slopes. Desert Indians used their red sap as medicine and to bring good fortune. Elephant trees are common to Baja California and the Mexican state of Sonora but are found in only a few scattered canyons and washes of Anza-Borrego—the northernmost extension of their range.

An easy, educational loop winds up and down a rock-lined wash with thirteen plant identification stops keyed to the brochure. Most of the plants are common desert perennial shrubs such as burroweed, desert lavender, and brittlebush. Certainly the most fascinating plant is the trail's namesake elephant tree, *Bursera microphylla*. The species name means "small-leaved," a common adaptation by desert plants to conserve water. The common name reflects the folded "skin" of the main trunk, much like that of an elephant.

12 Narrows Earth Trail

Offering insights into the geologic forces that created these mountains, this ½-mile loop features a self-guiding brochure that explains the fault lines of the gorge and the power of erosion along the edge of an alluvial fan. Chuparosa and pencil cholla abound.

Start: About 20 miles south of Borrego Springs.
Distance: 0.5-mile loop.
Approximate hiking time: Up to 1 hour.
Difficulty: Easy.
Trail surface: Dirt trail.

Seasons: October through May.
USGS topo map: Borrego Sink-CA (1:24,000).
Trail contact: Anza-Borrego Desert State Park (see appendix D).

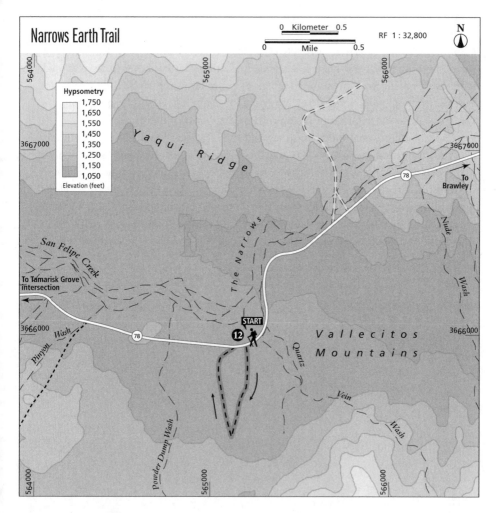

Finding the trailhead: From the park visitor center in Borrego Springs, go east on Palm Canyon Drive to Christmas Circle (1.9 miles); at the circle turn south onto Borrego Springs Road. Drive south-southeast 5.6 miles to the Y intersection; turn right onto S3. Go 7.4 miles to the intersection with California Highway 78 just beyond the Tamarisk Grove Campground. Turn left (east) on CA 78 and continue 4.7 miles to the Narrows Earth parking area, signed on your right. The parking area is a wide spot on the right side of CA 78 immediately before the road takes a sharp right-angle turn (north) through the Narrows.

The Hike

The trailhead for this short nature trail is on a busy state highway, a major through route for trucks. It is immediately west of a narrow gap (labeled "The Narrows" on the topographic map) where Yaqui Ridge almost meets the Vallecitos Mountains.

The signed, self-guided trail begins directly east of the parking area to your left. It's easy to miss spot no. 1, which is important since the brochures are located there. The points along the trail focus on the geologic history of the region, revealed in the naked rock walls of this canyon. Fault lines, rock formation, and erosion are some of the lessons of the Narrows Earth Trail. The seven stops on the loop provide an introduction to the forces that created Anza-Borrego topography.

From the top of the loop, Powder Dump Wash continues another 0.2 mile to a sharp rise. For a longer hike, and to apply your newly acquired knowledge, you can continue up the wash before returning to the parking area.

13 Kenyon Overlook Trail Loop

From a rocky ridge in the central region of the park, this short loop trail provides a panoramic vista. On a clear day the expansive view extends beyond the Vallecitos Mountains as far as the Salton Sea.

Start: About 13 miles south of Borrego Springs.
Distance: 1-mile loop.
Approximate hiking time: Less than 1 hour.
Difficulty: Easy.
Trail surface: Dirt path.

Seasons: October through April.
USGS topo map: Borrego Sink-CA (1:24,000).
Trail contact: Anza-Borrego Desert State Park (see appendix D).

Finding the trailhead: From the visitor center in Borrego Springs, go east on Palm Canyon Drive 1.9 miles to Christmas Circle. At the circle take Borrego Springs Road south for 5.6 miles to the Y intersection. At the Y turn right (south) onto S3 (Yaqui Pass Road). Drive 5.8 miles and turn left into the Yaqui Pass Primitive Campground, the northern trailhead.

After hiking the point-to-point loop trail to the Kenyon Overlook parking pullout, walk back down the highway about 0.2 mile to the starting point at the Yaqui Pass Campground parking lot.

Kenyon Overlook Trail Loop; Cactus Loop Trail; Yaqui Well Nature Trail

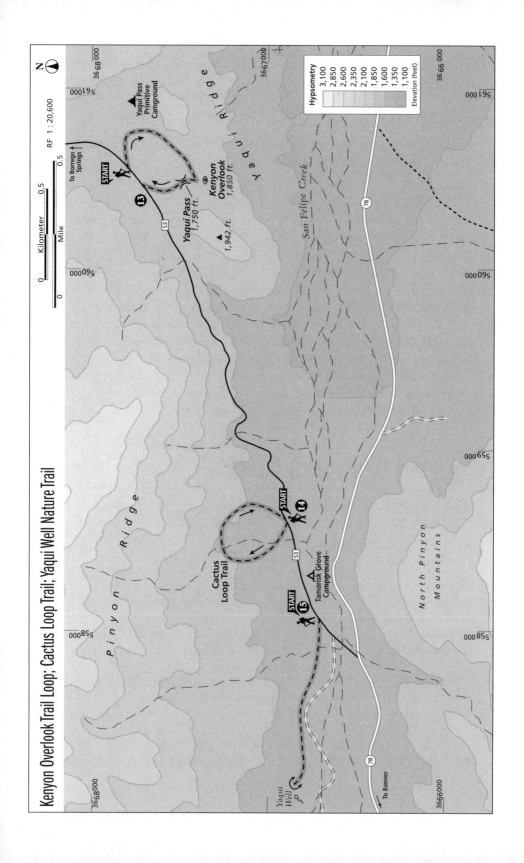

RF 1 : 20,600

Hypsometry

Elevation (feet)
3,100
2,850
2,600
2,350
2,100
1,850
1,600
1,350
1,100

Kilometer 0 0.5 0.5

Mile 0 0.5

N

To Borrego Springs

START 13

Yaqui Pass Primitive Campground

Yaqui Pass 1,750 ft.

Kenyon Overlook 1,850 ft.

1,942 ft.

Yaqui Ridge

San Felipe Creek

Pinyon Ridge

Cactus Loop Trail

START 14

S3

Tamarisk Grove Campground

START 15

78

North Pinyon Mountains

Yaqui Well

To Banner

78

Ocotillo (left) on the Kenyon Overlook trail.

The Hike

From the trailhead, take the signed trail uphill. The trail maintains a gentle up-and-down grade through a series of parallel gullies lined with yucca, creosote bushes, silver cholla, ocotillo, beavertail cacti, barrel cacti, and brittlebush. Soon the trail reaches the high point at a rocky ridge overlook. Turn left and walk about 30 yards to the overlook, which contains a monument in honor of William L. Kenyon, a noted desert conservationist and district park superintendent from 1947 to 1959. From here the desert spreads out like the pages of a book. Beyond is a seemingly endless series of *arroyos* (washes) that deposit gravel and silt in deltalike fans, two or more of which are called *bajadas*. These bajadas support a dense mantle of agave, called mescal. On a clear day the Salton Sea can be seen 30 miles to the east.

From the overlook, return to the main trail, turn left, and drop gradually to the highway, which can be seen from this point. Upon reaching the highway, make a right turn and walk 0.2 mile up the highway to the starting point at the Yaqui Pass Primitive Campground.

Trail

clustered along this nature trail, which is at a higher ele-
...rk; here you can find wildflowers blooming one or two
...Palm Canyon.

See map on page 48.
Start: About 15 miles south of Borrego
Springs.
Distance: 1-mile loop.
Approximate hiking time: Less than 1 hour.
Difficulty: Easy.

Trail surface: Dirt trail.
Seasons: October through April.
USGS topo map: Borrego Sink-CA
(1:24,000).
Trail contact: Anza-Borrego Desert State Park
(see appendix D).

Finding the trailhead: From the park visitor center in Borrego Springs, take Palm Canyon
Drive east to Christmas Circle. At the circle, take Borrego Springs Road (S3) south and go 5.6
miles to the Y intersection. Bear right and continue on S3 for 7 miles to Tamarisk Grove Campground, on your left. The signed Cactus Loop Trail trailhead is across from the campground
entrance. Park in the shade of the tamarisk trees along the south side of the highway.

The Hike

This short trail begins as a sandy winding path but becomes more rocky as it leads
up the canyon. Your self-guided-hike brochure identifies jumping cholla, beavertail
cactus, and saltbush. Walking up the canyon instead of driving the desert roads reveals
the diversity of desert plant life and its adaptive strategies for desert survival. The
nature trail route leads up the wash to the ridge's high point (1,520 feet) then winds
gently down the ridge slope to the trailhead on S3. The exit sign is obscured by
overgrown brittlebush, but the trail itself is clear.

15 Yaqui Well Nature Trail

The easy trail to Yaqui Well and back features a plethora of cacti and opportunities for birding at the watering hole.

See map on page 48.
Start: About 15 miles south of Borrego Springs.
Distance: 2 miles out and back.
Approximate hiking time: 1 hour.
Difficulty: Easy.

Trail surface: Clear trail.
Seasons: October through April.
USGS topo maps: Tubb Canyon-CA and Borrego Sink-CA (1:24,000).
Trail contact: Anza-Borrego Desert State Park (see appendix D).

Finding the trailhead: From the park visitor center in Borrego Springs, go east 1.9 miles to Christmas Circle. At the circle, turn south on Borrego Springs Road (S3). After 5.6 miles, at the Y intersection, bear right (south) on Yaqui Pass Road (also S3). Continue 7 miles to Tamarisk Grove Campground, which is across the road from Yaqui Well Nature Trail. Park along S3 outside the campground and cross the highway to the trailhead.

The Hike

This nature trail, slightly longer than most of the others in the park, has an informative brochure to accompany you on your walk. The route begins at the highway but quickly angles up a rise on a gentle but rocky trail, and the hiker becomes enveloped in the desert. The nature trail signs are frequent and are clearly situated so each plant is labeled correctly. Jumping cholla are the most numerous, but ironwood and desert mistletoe also appear here.

Approaching the well from the east, the trail becomes sandy and level for the last 0.6 mile. The foliage at the well provides a sharp contrast with the surrounding desert plants. A dense thicket of mesquite crowds around the watery seep. Hardy old mesquite and ironwood trees surround the area. The well is a popular watering spot for local animals, especially birds. Although you can drive to the well via the Yaqui Well Campground road, the walk through the desert makes the existence of this moisture more significant.

16 Wilson Trail

A long east–west trail that follows the old Pinyon Ridge jeep trail (closed to vehicular travel), passing by 4,573-foot Mount Wilson to arrive at a rocky overlook above Borrego Valley. This is one of the longer out-and-back hikes in the park, with sweeping vistas of the central park region.

Start: About 8 miles southwest of Borrego Springs.
Distance: 11 miles out and back.
Approximate hiking time: 5 to 7 hours.
Difficulty: Moderate.

Trail surface: Dirt trail.
Seasons: October through April.
USGS topo map: Tubb Canyon-CA (1:24,000).
Trail contact: Anza-Borrego Desert State Park (see appendix D).

Finding the trailhead: Go 15 miles east of Warner Springs, on Park Route S22 (Montezuma Valley Road); 10.5 miles east of the intersection with S2 or 8 miles southwest of the park visitor center in Borrego Springs, take the Culp Valley Road south. Four-wheel-drive vehicles are recommended on this steep, sandy road. After 0.4 mile stay right at the first road junction. Continue on the main road, ignoring numerous turnouts. The Wilson trailhead is another 2.7 miles up the road, for a total of 3.1 miles from S22, and is marked by a small sign with a turnaround parking area just below a ridge dotted with sage, creosote, and granite boulders.

The Hike

The trail climbs moderately the first 0.6 mile to the ridgetop, opening up panoramic vistas of the Vallecito Mountains to the southeast. It then gradually descends another 0.5 mile to a broad saddle adorned with a heavy mantle of juniper, cholla, and agave. After another 0.4 mile this former jeep trail tops out on a high ridge with an outcrop of sparkling light-colored granite boulders just to the right. This sandy track then levels, climbs, and levels again for another mile. In a few places the trail is somewhat overgrown by vegetation, but all you have to do is look ahead 50 yards or so and you'll easily spot the remnants of the two-track jeep trail.

At this point the trail climbs steeply 0.2 mile, weaving between large boulders, then drops 0.1 mile, followed by a steep 0.2-mile climb to a high side ridge. It then drops slightly and levels out for 1 mile. Soon the ridge is sprinkled with a few piñon pines and cedar adding variety to the mix of high-desert flora.

The old jeep trail appears to end after 5 miles and after climbing gradually to a downed post with a cement base. A more primitive path marked by rock cairns leads steeply up through thick brush for about 0.2 mile. The path tops out in a saddle between the rocky points, including 4,573-foot Mount Wilson, and continues across a broad, open plateau for another 0.3 mile. Here the sandy path disappears as the slope begins to drop eastward.

Wilson Trail

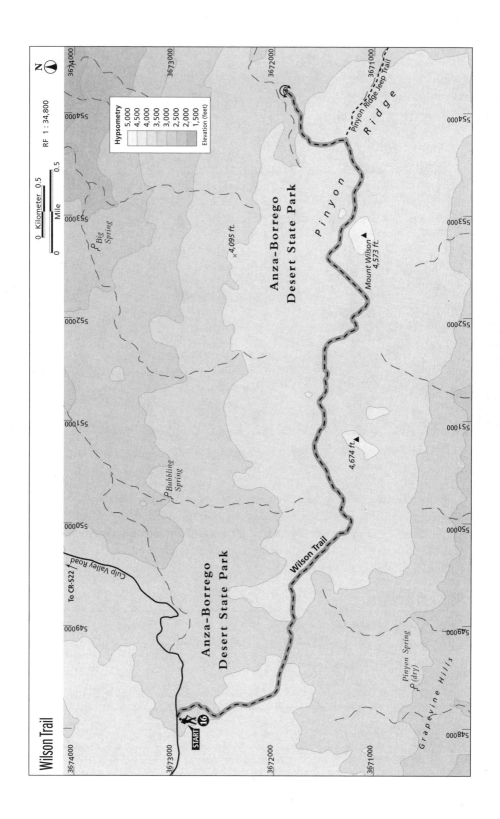

Anza-Borrego Desert State Park

Anza-Borrego Desert State Park

Wilson Trail

To CR-S22

Culp Valley Road

START **16**

Big Spring

Bubbling Spring

× 4,095 ft.

4,674 ft. ▲

Mount Wilson 4,573 ft. ▲

Pinyon Ridge Jeep Trail

Pinyon Ridge

Pinyon Spring (dry)

Grapevine Hills

Hypsometry

5,000
4,500
4,000
3,500
3,000
2,500
2,000
1,500

Elevation (feet)

0 Kilometer 0.5
0 Mile 0.5

RF 1 : 34,800

N

The Wilson Trail follows the high ridge near the halfway point.

Before heading back to the trailhead, walk about 100 yards north to the rock-lined lip of the ridge for a stunning view of Borrego Springs, the Salton Sea, and surrounding desert basins and ranges fading far into the distance. This remote stretch of the Grapevine Hills is used extensively by mountain lions, bobcats, and coyotes as evidenced by abundant scat along the trail.

Miles and Directions

0.0 Start at the trailhead.

5.0 The old jeep trail disappears; the primitive dirt trail continues.

5.5 The use trail disappears. Hike north to the overlook.

11.0 Return to the trailhead.

17 California Riding and Hiking Trail: Peña Spring and Culp Valley Overlook

This maintained section of the Riding and Hiking Trail is almost entirely downhill. It goes by Peña Spring, includes the Culp Valley Overlook, then descends to the valley floor and a cross-desert walk to the visitor center in Borrego Springs. Along the way you may enjoy views of Borrego Valley, Coyote Mountain, and the Santa Rosa Mountains.

Start: About 8 miles southwest of Borrego Springs.
Distance: 8.5 miles one way.
Approximate hiking time: 4 to 5 hours.
Difficulty: Strenuous.

Trail surface: Dirt trail except for some overgrown portions of the less-traveled section above Culp Valley Overlook.
Seasons: October through April.
USGS topo map: Tubb Canyon-CA (1:24,000).
Trail contact: Anza-Borrego Desert State Park (see appendix D).

Finding the trailhead: A small sign marks the trailhead 12 miles east of Warner Springs on Park Route S22 (Montezuma Valley Road), 6.8 miles east of Park Route S2. The trailhead is on the north side of the road. This point is 10 miles southwest of the visitor center in Borrego Springs.

The destination point for the car shuttle is the visitor center. Horse parties end their trip at a parking pullout at mile 16 on S22, 1 mile south. Hikers may also prefer this convenient destination since it eliminates a dry 1-mile walk across the valley floor.

The Hike

The California Riding and Hiking Trail spans the varied elevations of Anza-Borrego. Beginning at 4,000 feet in chaparral, it descends through mountain valleys to the desert floor. The transition of vegetative communities is as interesting as the view—and the trip down the ridge offers spectacular vistas.

As you drive to the trailhead, the length and the elevation gain of Montezuma Road may be intimidating. The trail is nowhere near as arduous as the drive up! The trail avoids the rocky ridges you see from the road. Although there is little horse use on the trail due to steepness, neither is this a bighorn-sheep trail.

The early section of trail is the most difficult to find since it is not used often and is overgrown with chaparral. Stay within 50 yards north of the road, and watch for yellow-topped posts hidden by aggressive shrubbery. You can see this peekaboo trail better by looking ahead about 50 yards. This section is not used frequently, compared with the last 5 miles of the hike, east of Culp Valley. Close to

A large multistemmed cholla stands like a giant candelabra next to the California R&H Trail.

the Montezuma-Borrego Highway (S22), you may pick up traffic noise, but as you wind north of rock outcroppings and ridges, that fades. Soon you are surrounded by wild country.

At the midsection of the hike, the trail goes through Culp Valley, an area formerly used for grazing cattle. Traces of its ranching past are noticeable—such as the stock watering facilities you will spot to your left. Peña Spring, now barely a seep, creates a patch of greenery in the high valley before you climb to the Culp Valley Overlook. This section of the trail is easily accessible to the highway, with a parking area. Frequently visitors take the 0.5-mile hike to enjoy the view. Thus, more signs mark the trail. Apparently more hikers also start the journey here: The trail is more heavily used from this point to the valley below.

Although the Culp Valley Overlook itself is prominently marked with a sign, there are dozens of breathtaking overlooks on the descent to the valley. Don't use up your film on the first one you come to! This 5-mile section will provide many photo opportunities. The trail goes down a series of giant stair steps—sharp descents followed by small landings, each one hosting a cactus display and stunning diversity of

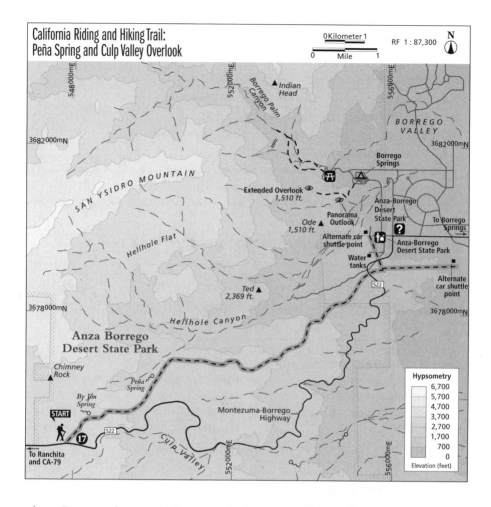

0 Kilometer 1

RF 1 : 87,300

N

0   Mile   1

Indian
Head

BORREGO
VALLEY

Borrego
Springs

Extended Overlook 1,510 ft.

Panorama
Outlook

Ode ▲
1,510 ft.

Anza-Borrego
Desert
State Park

To Borrego
Springs

SAN YSIDRO MOUNTAIN

Hellhole Flat

Alternate car
shuttle point

Anza-Borrego
Desert State Park

Water
tanks

S22

Ted ▲
2,369 ft.

Alternate
car shuttle
point

Hellhole Canyon

Anza Borrego
Desert State Park

Chimney
Rock ▲

Peña
Spring

By Jim
Spring

START

Montezuma-Borrego
Highway

17

S22

Culp Valley

To Ranchita
and CA-79

Hypsometry	
	6,700
	5,700
	4,700
	3,700
	2,700
	1,700
	700
	0
Elevation (feet)	

plants. Between these sandy flat cactus gardens, the trail drops sharply, often via rocky gullies. Even with the town of Borrego Springs spreading out below, you'll have a genuine sense of seclusion; the busy highway to Borrego Springs is beyond the ridge to the south.

Upon reaching the valley floor, you can follow the wide trail to your right to the parking area/trailhead created for horse users. This is a convenient place for a car shuttle. To return to the visitor center complex or the adjacent campground, go straight north from the end of the hillside trail. Trying to find a marked trail on the desert floor is time consuming and unnecessary, since you can see the rooftops of the park buildings immediately to the north. Use the highly visible tree-encircled water tanks as an intermediate guide. The visitor center is 0.3 mile beyond the tanks.

If your driver is late meeting you after your hike, waiting at the visitor center may be a more attractive option than waiting at the parking lot on S22.

Miles and Directions

0.0–0.4 Watch for yellow-topped posts in this overgrown section.

0.4 The trail stops: Head for the saddle on a low ridge.

0.5 Stay left of the wash as the trail skirts the small valley.

0.7 Watch for a primitive stock tank on the hillside (left).

1.2–1.7 You'll see signs at trail intersections at the Culp Valley Overlook area.

1.7–7.5 The trail descends into the valley.

7.5–8.5 There's a 1-mile trailless hike to the visitor center. A marked wash (right) leads to the parking lot for parties on horseback.

18 Panorama Overlook/Extended Overlook

This short but steep climb via a switchback trail up San Ysidro Mountain provides a scenic overlook of Borrego Valley. By continuing higher, you gain an even more expansive view point.

Start: Just west of the campground near the Borrego Springs Visitor Center.
Distance: 2.6 miles out and back.
Approximate hiking time: 3 to 5 hours.
Difficulty: Strenuous.
Trail surface: Rocky trail to overlook; steep rocky use trail to extended overlook.

Seasons: October through April.
USGS topo map: Borrego Palms Canyon-CA (1:24,000).
Trail contact: Anza-Borrego Desert State Park (see appendix D).

Finding the trailhead: From the visitor center at the intersection of Park Route S22 and Palm Canyon Drive in Borrego Springs, follow signs north 0.8 mile to the Borrego Springs Campground. The trail starts near campsite no. 71. A level 1-mile trail from the visitor center northwest to the campground also intersects the Panorama Overlook Trail.

The Hike

From the signed trailhead next to the palm tree at campsite no. 71, take the trail across a flat alluvial fan along the base of the rocky hillside for 0.4 mile to the OVER-LOOK TRAIL sign where the trail begins to switchback up the slope. The clear but steep and rocky trail climbs 240 feet over a distance of 0.3 mile to an open knoll ringed by creosote bushes, offering a wide vista from the eastern foot of San Ysidro Mountain to Borrego Palm Canyon and Borrego Valley.

For an even more expansive view, continue west up the ridge on a use trail, well defined for the first 0.2 mile as it follows the initial level portion of the ridge. The use trail then winds upward through rocks and brush and sometimes all but

Indian Head Mountain glimpsed from the extended Panorama Overlook.

disappears. Simply follow the main crest of the ridge leading toward the distant summit of San Ysidro Mountain. At times the best footing is found along either side of the actual ridgeline.

After another 0.4 mile and 300-foot gain, you'll reach a somewhat level rocky ledge with several flat spots. These make for a wonderful extended overlook—a good place to sit and soak up the majestic desert scenery of canyons, alluvial fans, mountains, valleys, and jagged, exposed ridges. The palm groves of Borrego Palm Canyon are hidden from view, but take time here to scan the slopes for desert bighorn sheep. As with most mountainous use trails, this one is easier to find going down than up.

This extended overlook is a logical turnaround point for a vigorous half-day hike, although it is possible to scramble up the ridge another 4 or 5 miles to the lofty summit of 6,147-foot San Ysidro Peak on the park's western boundary. This would be a very strenuous full-day cross-country climb with more than a vertical mile of gain and loss. Many overly optimistic day hikers have mistakenly spent a cold night on this mountain, usually giving rise to search and rescue operations. Know your limits.

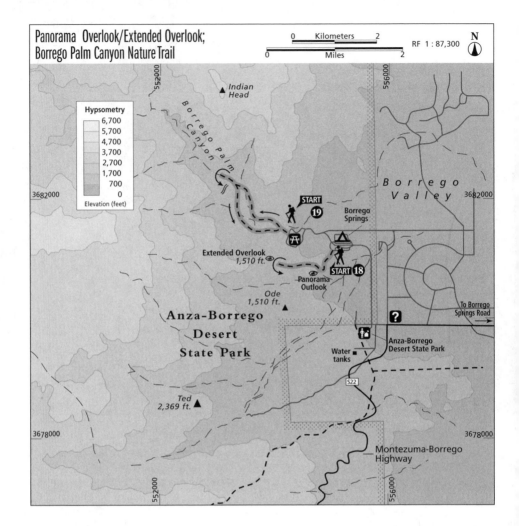

Panorama Overlook/Extended Overlook;
Borrego Palm Canyon Nature Trail

Miles and Directions

0.0 Start at the trailhead at campsite no. 71.

0.4 The switchback trail begins here.

0.7 Reach the Panorama Overlook (1,020 feet).

1.3 End the hike at the extended overlook (1,510 feet).

2.6 Return to the trailhead.

19 Borrego Palm Canyon Nature Trail

What was once a delightful series of palm groves and mountain oases in the park, and the most heavily visited trail, has now become instead an example of the transitory nature of life in the desert. A torrential storm in the mountains above the canyon caused a "one-hundred-year" flash flood in September 2004 and washed away over half the palm trees and most of the trail. Life goes on: The sheep for whom the park is named are sometimes spotted on canyon slopes above the oasis.

See map on page 60.
Start: 0.6 mile north of the visitor center in Borrego Springs.
Distance: 3.5-mile loop.
Approximate hiking time: 1 to 2 hours.
Difficulty: Moderate rock scramble to the oasis and to the canyon overlook.

Trail surface: Washed out; rocky temporary path, flagged and with cairns.
Seasons: October through April.
USGS topo map: Borrego Palm Canyon-CA (1:24,000).
Trail contact: Anza-Borrego Desert State Park (see appendix D).

Finding the trailhead: From the park visitor center in Borrego Springs, go north 1 mile on an access road to Borrego Palm Canyon Campground and Picnic Area. The trail leaves from the northwest end of the picnic area. There is a day-use fee to enter with a motor vehicle.

The Hike

This trail provides a spectacular introduction to the beauty and fragility of the desert. A pond with desert pupfish lies at the start of the trail. Ocotillos abound, as do mesquite, cheesebush, and chuparosa, the "hummingbird plant." Hummingbirds are plentiful, especially in spring. In winter and spring, water flows in the adjacent stream, with small waterfalls. Sharp-eyed hikers can often spot bighorn sheep on the mountain slopes of the canyon, especially in early morning or evening.

Since September 2004 the walk up the trail into the canyon has changed radically. The trail winds through large boulders to what was once one of the largest groves of California fan palms in the country. A short but steeper climb above the oasis leads to an overlook 30 feet above the streambed.

On the way out an alternate route goes along the higher canyon slope to the west, amid a slope of ocotillos. This route also leads back to the parking lot; it is slightly longer (0.5 mile more) and more strenuous (100 feet elevation gain) than the path along the stream. But you also enjoy a loftier view of the canyon mouth below and you get a bigger picture of the devastating flood.

Miles and Directions

0.0 There's a pupfish pond located at the trailhead.

1.5 You'll see the remains of a palm oasis.

1.75 There's an overlook above the oasis.

3.5 Return to the trailhead.

20 Alcoholic Pass

A sweeping vista of the northeastern section of Anza–Borrego is your reward for climbing to Alcoholic Pass.

Start: About 8 miles north of Borrego Springs.
Distance: 3.4 miles out and back.
Approximate hiking time: 2 to 3 hours.
Difficulty: Moderate.
Trail surface: Dirt trail, rocky wash.

Seasons: October through April.
USGS topo maps: Borrego Palm Canyon-CA and Clark Lake-CA (1:24,000).
Trail contact: Anza-Borrego Desert State Park (see appendix D).

Finding the trailhead: From the park visitor center in Borrego Springs, go east on Palm Canyon Drive 1.9 miles to Christmas Circle; continue 0.6 mile past the circle and turn north (left) on DiGiorgio Road. At 5 miles the pavement ends; continue north on Coyote Canyon Road, a rolling, soft dirt road, for 2.6 miles to the trailhead on your right.

The Hike

For centuries Alcoholic Pass has been used by the region's inhabitants to travel from Clark Valley (in the northeast) to Borrego Valley. These use trails were created by countless moccasins before our hiking boots arrived. As you climb to the pass, with its sweeping view, you can develop many theories about the origin of the pass's name.

The hike takes off for the first 0.2 mile up a sandy slope to a trail marker indicating a right turn up a sidehill; the trail follows this ridge up a moderate incline. It becomes progressively rockier as it climbs to the trip register at 1 mile. At that point you have reached a sandy plateau with sweeping views of the San Ysidro Mountains to the west and the Santa Rosa Mountains through the pass to the east.

The winding flat trail continues beyond the register, soon turning upward and becoming more boulder-strewn. At the summit of the pass, it opens into a wide sandy wash sloping northeast down to the plateau above Clark Valley. About 0.6 mile

Native California fan palm grove at the Borrego Palm Oasis.

Eastward below Alcoholic Pass toward the Santa Rosa Mountains.

beyond the pass, the wash opens into a high fan, spreading northeastward. This is a good spot to find a shady rock for lunch and/or contemplation before heading back to the trailhead.

Miles and Directions

0.0   From the trailhead, the well-traveled trail heads northeast.

0.2   The trail climbs a ridge.

0.3   The trail steepens sharply.

1.0   The register is located west of the pass itself.

1.1   This pass is a turnaround point. Retrace your steps to the trailhead for the shorter hike option.

1.7   This is the turnaround point for the longer trip option.

3.4   Return to the trailhead.

Alcoholic Pass

RF 1 : 33,600

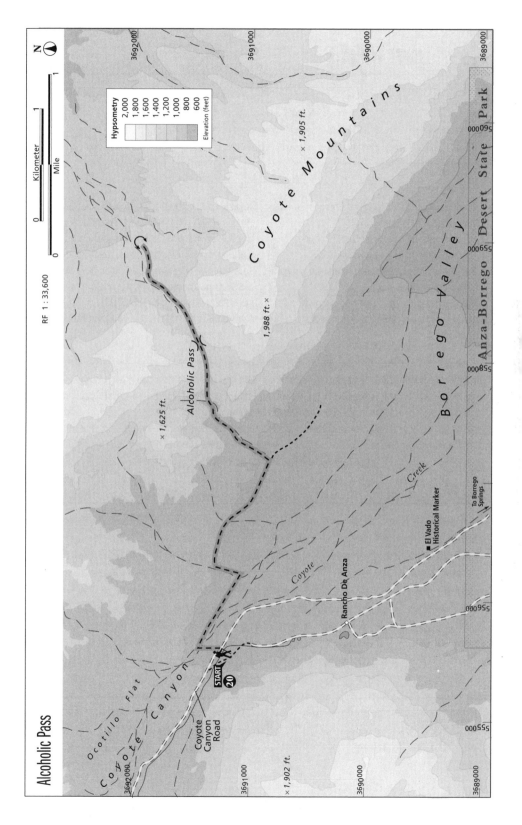

Coyote Mountains

Borrego Valley

Anza-Borrego Desert State Park

Ocotillo Flat

Coyote Canyon

Alcoholic Pass

× 1,625 ft.

× 1,988 ft.

× 1,905 ft.

× 1,902 ft.

Coyote Creek

Coyote Canyon Road

START 20

Rancho De Anza

El Vado Historical Marker

To Borrego Springs

Hypsometry
2,000
1,800
1,600
1,400
1,200
1,000
800
600
Elevation (feet)

N

Kilometer
0   1

Mile
0   1

3692000
3691000
3690000

3692000
3691000
3690000
3689000

555000
556000
558000
559000
560000
3689000

21 Lower Willows

This soggy, nearly flat hike out and back along Coyote Canyon Creek follows the historic Anza expedition route. Coyote Canyon Road is gated and the canyon is closed to visitors from June 1 to September 30 to protect bighorn-sheep access to water. In winter many birds can be spotted in the lush near-jungle setting of willow thickets, so bring your binoculars.

Start: About 9 miles north of Borrego Springs.
Distance: 4-mile loop.
Approximate hiking time: 2 to 5 hours, depending on distance.
Difficulty: Moderate (due to constant slogging through muck and water).
Trail surface: Dirt path with some rocky and muddy spots; possible stream crossings, so wear old boots.

Seasons: November through May. The trail is cleared each year the week before Thanksgiving; hikers are advised not to use the trail before then as it is generally impenetrable due to overgrown vegetation or erosion from floods.
USGS topo maps: Collins Valley-CA and Borrego Palm Canyon-CA (1:24,000).
Trail contact: Anza-Borrego Desert State Park (see appendix D).

Finding the trailhead: From the park visitor center in Borrego Springs, go east 1.9 miles on Palm Canyon Drive to Christmas Circle; continue east 0.6 mile and turn north (left) onto DiGiorgio Road. Drive north 5 miles until the pavement ends. Continue on unpaved Coyote Canyon Road 5 miles northwest to the Second Crossing (signed). The road is deeply eroded beyond this point, so those with low-clearance vehicles should park here, wade the stream, and walk up Coyote Canyon Road 0.7 mile to the trailhead. The Lower Willows Loop begins on the other side of the stream, about 100 yards past the Third Crossing (signed).

The Hike

The hike up Lower Willows is certain to be a memorable one. In the middle of this arid landscape, the trail follows the stream—along it, across it, in it. The well-signed trail is also used by equestrians since it provides access to Collins Valley and upper Coyote Canyon. The use by horses contributes to the muddy quality of the trail. Posted signs remind hikers that this is a fragile area and it is necessary to stay on the trail, which is often the streambed itself.

For years the Lower Willows streambed was also a roadbed. The Anza expeditions came along this route. The second one, in 1775, came through with a group of 240 settlers and 800 livestock. The water was a welcome relief for the party, but the impact on the riparian zone must have been enormous.

The trail zigzags upstream through dense willow saplings. After this muddy experience, the trail emerges in a wide, dry, sandy wash and the beginning of Middle Willows. At this point, follow the yellow-topped white posts up the bank to the west. On the horizon across Collins Valley, a prominent flat-topped mountain is an

Lower Willows; Indian Canyon; Cougar Canyon; Sheep Canyon

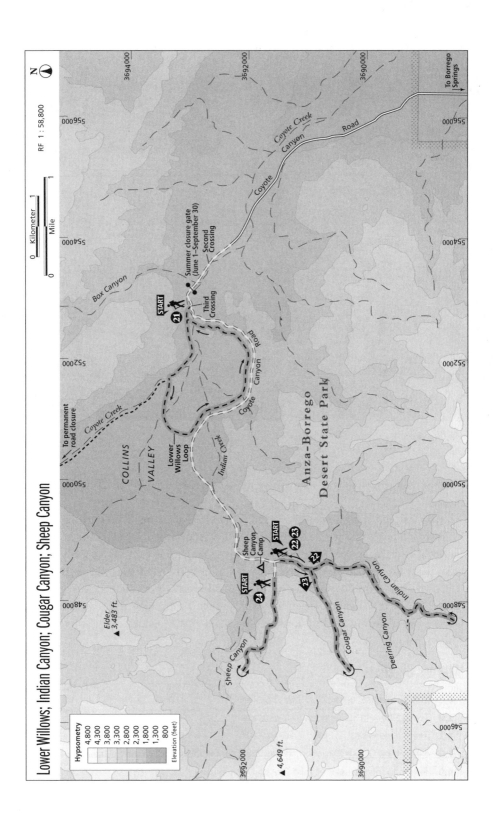

Wading the soggy Lower Willows Trail.

ideal beacon, helping you maintain your westward bearings to Coyote Canyon Road.

Turn left and follow this very rough four-wheel-drive road back to the Lower Willows trailhead. On weekends especially, this section of road is a favorite of the four-wheel-drive crowd. A couple of dicey spots in the canyons challenge even high-clearance vehicles. Be cautious in these spots and give drivers a wide berth.

Note: This section of the park is closed to all visitors from June 1 through September 30 so the bighorn sheep and other species can enjoy the scarce water of Coyote Creek during the hot summer. The gated closure is located right before the Third Crossing.

Miles and Directions

0.0 The trail begins just beyond Third Crossing.

1.0 Emerge from the streambed to a wide wash.

1.1 The trail goes west.

1.9 Turn left on Coyote Canyon Road (dirt road) for the route back to the trailhead.

4.0 Return to the trailhead at Third Crossing.

22 Indian Canyon

This hidden canyon with palm groves and lush vegetation was hit by flooding in 2004. The road to the trailhead has been heavily eroded; contact the park for an update on road conditions before embarking on your outing.

See map on page 67.
Start: About 15 miles northwest of Borrego Springs.
Distance: 4.5 miles out and back if you can drive to the trailhead (11.5 miles if you hike from Third Crossing; 12.5 miles if you hike from Second Crossing).
Approximate hiking time: 3 to 8 hours, depending on how far you can drive.
Difficulty: Strenuous due to eroded trail.

Trail surface: Rocky path, becoming more primitive as you climb.
Seasons: November through April. Coyote Canyon is closed to human visitors from June 1 through September 30 to protect bighorn-sheep access to water sources.
USGS topo map: Borrego Palm Canyon-CA (1:24,000).
Trail contact: Anza-Borrego Desert State Park (see appendix D).

Finding the trailhead: From the visitor center in Borrego Springs, go east 1.9 miles on Palm Canyon Drive to Christmas Circle; continue 0.6 mile beyond the circle to a left turn on DiGiorgio Road. Drive 5 miles to the end of the pavement, then continue north on unpaved Coyote Canyon Road. The first crossing of the stream is not difficult under normal conditions. The Second Crossing may pose a problem for vehicles with low clearance; if so, park there and hike the rest of the way. The distance from the Second Crossing to the Indian Canyon trailhead is approximately 4.6 miles. After the Third Crossing, even high-clearance vehicles may have difficulty. The road beyond that point requires very high clearance, four-wheel drive, and enormous courage. Park near the stream and hike from there.

The hike follows the road, so be careful about traffic, especially on weekends. After you climb the rise to the floor of Collins Valley, you'll see a well-marked section of a horse trail (left) that shortens the trip and avoids road traffic. The actual trailhead is at a parking area 0.1 mile south of the Sheep Canyon road junction where a sign indicates Indian and Cougar Canyons to the south and Sheep Canyon to the west.

The Hike

This hike in Indian Canyon has no convenient road access if your vehicle is not suitable for rough terrain. But this verdant canyon hike is well worth the walk to the trailhead. The stream flow will be reduced in the fall, but the greenery will still be striking.

From the trailhead, the wide trail goes south up the sloping valley floor, surrounded by creosote. When the trail enters the canyon, you may notice damage caused by flooding in 2004. The lush riparian zone was remodeled by the flood. The use trail weaves back and forth across the eroded stream as it goes up the valley. Decades of hiking explorers have created a maze of pathways, which, compounded with the flood damage, make route-finding challenging. The trail becomes faint in

This lone palm tree stands in the Valley of the Thousand Springs in Indian Canyon.

places, but persistent hikers can pick a route by focusing on a distant goal, such as a grove of palm trees.

Heading up the valley through the cobweb of trails, you eventually arrive at a lone palm (0.3 mile from the canyon mouth) at the foot of a slender ridge that marks the confluence of two drainages: Deering Canyon on the west and Indian Canyon on the south. A trail leads to the top of the ridge, from which you gain a panoramic view of this inner valley. Up Deering Canyon, a stair-step palm grove leads up its steep drainage. Sycamores line the more gentle Indian Canyon to the left. Both of these options are worthy of further exploration, although the trail becomes less defined in either direction. Enjoy this remote wilderness before retracing your steps to the trailhead.

Note: If you plan to spend the night in Indian Canyon, remember the park policy regarding camping near water sources. To ensure the nocturnal animals' access to water, it is essential that you camp at least 200 yards from the stream. Remember, too, that all human travel in Coyote Canyon is forbidden from June 1 through September 30; the closure is at the Third Crossing of Coyote Creek.

Miles and Directions

0.0 Start at the Cougar Canyon/Indian Canyon trailhead.

0.5 Continue south at the faded trail signpost where Cougar Canyon goes right.

0.9 The trail hugs the hillside to the right and enters the canyon.

1.8 There's a lone palm at the canyon junction. Deering Canyon is west, while Indian Canyon continues south.

2.25 Continue south into Indian Canyon.

4.5 Turn around and return to the trailhead. (**Note:** It's an 11.5-mile round-trip from Third Crossing and 12.5-mile round-trip from Second Crossing.)

23 Cougar Canyon

If you can drive to the trailhead, Cougar Canyon is a moderate hike up a sloping canyon floor in bighorn-sheep habitat. The trail becomes progressively more primitive as you climb into the canyon.

See map on page 67.
Start: About 15 miles northwest of Borrego Springs.
Distance: 3 miles out and back if you can drive to the trailhead (10 miles if you hike from the Third Crossing of Coyote Creek; 11 miles if you hike from Second Crossing).
Approximate hiking time: 2 hours from canyon mouth.
Difficulty: Moderate from canyon mouth; strenuous for longer hike.

Trail surface: Dirt trail, eroded in places, fading to primitive as you climb.
Seasons: November through April. Coyote Canyon is closed June 1 through September 30 to protect bighorn-sheep access to water sources.
USGS topo map: Borrego Palm Canyon-CA (1:24,000).
Trail contact: Anza-Borrego Desert State Park (see appendix D).

Finding the trailhead: From the Borrego Springs visitor center, go east on Palm Canyon Drive 1.9 miles to Christmas Circle; continue 0.6 mile beyond the circle to left turn on DiGiorgio Road. Drive north on DiGiorgio Road 5 miles until the pavement ends. Continue north 5 miles on Coyote Canyon Road, a primitive but passable route, to the parking area before the Second Crossing (marked with a sign, and also the site of a gauging station). Depending on the water level and clearance of your vehicle, you can also drive to park after the Third Crossing. The road beyond that point requires very high clearance, four-wheel drive, and enormous courage.

The hike from the Second Crossing is about 4.6 miles to the Cougar Canyon/Sheep Canyon junction sign; from the Third Crossing, it is about 4 miles to the junction sign. Follow the jeep road from the crossing, but take the equestrian trail to your left when you reach Collins Valley for a more direct route and to avoid motorized traffic on the road, especially on weekends. From the junction sign, follow the road another 0.1 mile to the Indian Canyon/Cougar Canyon trailhead.

The Hike

This canyon journey is a delightful surprise, not only because of the lengthy hike just to get here, but also because the area's wonders are hidden from view even when you finally arrive at the canyon mouth. Have faith, and keep on hiking.

After Collins Valley and the dry lower reaches of Indian Canyon, the turnoff to Cougar Canyon seems like just another arid desert valley. Then, as you round the bend in the lower reaches of the canyon, your ears may detect the tinkling of a waterfall. Your eyes will be astounded with the lush riparian area. Sandy beaches and inviting pools dot the watercourse down the canyon, all reached by a labyrinth of trails that wind around boulders. Sycamores and palm trees are scattered along the stream bank above rock-lined grottos. Plan on taking time to explore and enjoy this rare water wonderland before your return trip. Some changes to the canyon occurred in the fall-of-2004 flash flood. The canyon floor was scoured in places and some of the trees were swept away. The desert is the scene of dramatic changes!

The stream may be only a trickle in the fall, but the vegetation will still provide a colorful contrast with the rest of Collins Valley. If you plan to camp overnight, remember the park regulations about water sources. Since desert wildlife is largely nocturnal, considerate campers don't obstruct animals' access to water. Camp at least 200 yards away from the stream.

Note: The summer closure of Coyote Canyon, from June 1 through September 30, makes this outing off-limits during that season.

Miles and Directions

0.0 The trail goes south from the Cougar Canyon/Indian Canyon trailhead.

0.5 At the trail junction, a faded sign indicates the Cougar Canyon trail to the right.

1.5 The trail fades as it climbs.

3.0 Retrace your steps to the trailhead. (**Note:** Round-trip from Third Crossing is 10 miles, from Second Crossing 11 miles.)

◀ *The stream in Cougar Canyon brings a swath of greenery to an arid landscape.*

24 Sheep Canyon

A primitive hike through a lush canyon with year-round pools of water, and an optional tough side trip to an idyllic waterfall, Sheep Canyon is a stark contrast to the surrounding desert. You also will see evidence of the 2004 flood that radically altered the landscape.

See map on page 67.
Start: About 15 miles northwest of Borrego Springs.
Distance: 3 miles out and back if you drive to the trailhead (11 miles if you hike from the Second Crossing on Coyote Canyon Road).
Approximate hiking time: 2 hours; 5 hours for longer hike.
Difficulty: Strenuous.
Trail surface: Primitive dirt and rock trail with trailless sections on and above the canyon floor.

Seasons: November through April. The area above Lower Willows, which includes Collins Valley/Sheep Canyon, is closed to human visitors from June 1 through September 30 to protect bighorn-sheep access to water sources.
USGS topo map: Borrego Palm Canyon-CA (1:24,000).
Trail contact: Anza-Borrego Desert State Park (see appendix D).

Finding the trailhead: From the park visitor center in Borrego Springs, drive east 1.9 miles on Palm Canyon Drive to Christmas Circle; continue 0.6 mile beyond the circle and make a left turn on DiGiorgio Road. Drive 5 miles to the end of the pavement, then continue north on unpaved Coyote Canyon Road. The first wash crossing is normally not difficult. The Second Crossing may stop low-clearance vehicles. If stopped, park and continue on foot up the Coyote Canyon Road. The road distance from the Second Crossing to the Sheep Canyon trailhead is approximately 4.6 miles. After the Third Crossing, even four-wheel-drive, high-clearance vehicles may be stopped at the foot of an extremely steep, rocky stretch of the road.

While hiking the road, be on the lookout for four-wheel-drive vehicles, especially on weekends. After climbing to the floor of Collins Valley, veer left on a well-marked horse trail that shortens the distance and avoids vehicular traffic. Upon reaching the signed Cougar Canyon/Sheep Canyon road junction, turn right (northwest) and proceed another 0.25 mile to the official trailhead at the primitive camp near the mouth of Sheep Canyon.

The Hike

Water flows through the rugged confines of Sheep Canyon during most of the year, although the canyon is apt to be dry by the time autumn rolls around. Depending on the season, a bubbling stream flows down steep rocks into deep pools lined by shady grottos. A few palm trees scattered along the brushy cottonwood-sycamore bottom make this twisting gorge a true desert oasis. A primitive on-again/off-again use trail winds up the lower reaches of Sheep Canyon into the North Fork. The "one-hundred-year" flood of 2004 has rearranged the terrain in Sheep Canyon, as well as in the other canyons in the northern part of the park.

Small waterfalls and deep pools are among the surprises in the remote North Fork of Sheep Canyon.

From the primitive camp the rock-lined trail immediately crosses the wash. The trail crosses the stream several times before working up a side ridge at 0.4 mile near the South Fork, which joins the main Sheep Canyon from the left. The South Fork is one of the steepest, roughest canyons in the park and should only be traversed by well-conditioned, experienced rock scramblers. It is possible to take a short but strenuous side trip by entering the South Fork at mile 0.4. The next 0.3 mile consists of gaining 350 feet through heavy brush and over rock slabs to the base of an idyllic 30-foot waterfall overseen by a small palm grove.

After enjoying this sublime setting, double-back to the main canyon and continue up the left side of the North Fork. Shortly, the trail crosses the stream to the right side in a dense mixture of palm and sycamore trees. Within 0.2 mile a huge boulder blocks the trail. Before climbing over the boulder, savor the music of rushing water and the stillness of the deep canyon.

At 0.7 mile the trail drops to several gigantic boulders that form a cavern. Back-track about 30 yards to a faint path that climbs between the boulders. Maneuver under and around several rock overhangs to follow the most prominent path, which soon crosses over to the left side of the canyon. This is a scenic alcove, with palm trees wedged in a narrow rock chute surrounded by the geologic faulting of tilted rock beds. The trail pitches steeply upward before dropping to the palm grove.

At 1 mile the trail again descends, this time to a lovely pool. Climb the stair-step rock to the left of the pool, soon reaching an overlook above a "weeping" rock where running water fans out across the face of a wall. Continue up the rough, rocky slope to a level shelf where a noticeable trail is again picked up. At 1.2 miles the canyon narrows, with bedded rock rising above two palm trees at 2,150 feet.

At 1.5 miles any resemblance to a trail vanishes near a lovely series of pools nestled beneath tall palms and sycamores. Extremely steep, loose, granitic side slopes demand slow and careful route-finding from this point on. This is a good turnaround point for a 3-mile round-trip sampler of the wild beauty of the North Fork of Sheep Canyon.

Miles and Directions

0.0 The primitive camp trailhead is near the mouth of Sheep Canyon.

0.4 The South Fork enters from the left; continue right up the main North Fork.

1.0 The trail reaches a deep pool just below a "weeping" rock wall.

1.5 The primitive trail disappears, making this a good turnaround point.

3.0 Return to the trailhead. (**Note:** It's an 11-mile round-trip from the Second Crossing, a 10-mile round-trip from the Third Crossing.)

25 Pacific Crest Trail: Table Mountain and Combs Peak

These two out-and-back day hikes take you through colorful canyons and chaparral/woodlands. You can reach some prominent peaks along these remote stretches of the Pacific Crest Trail (PCT).

Start: About 70 miles northwest of Borrego Springs.
Distance: Southern segment, 5 miles out and back to Combs Peak; Northern segment, 5 miles out and back to Table Mountain.
Approximate hiking time: 3 to 5 hours.
Difficulty: Strenuous to Combs Peak; moderate to Table Mountain.

Trail surface: Dirt and rocky trail; short off-trail route-finding climbs to both summits.
Seasons: October through May.
USGS topo map: Bucksnort Mountain-CA (1:24,000).
Trail contact: Anza-Borrego Desert State Park (see appendix D).

Finding the trailhead: To reach the Southern segment, take California Highway 79. About 3.3 miles south of Oak Grove and 10.8 miles north of Warner Springs, turn east on Chihuahua Road. After 6.5 miles the paved road curves right. Continue straight ahead to the end of the pavement and the beginning of the dirt Lost Valley Road. Continue past the biological station gate at 1.7 miles, reaching the park boundary at 3.1 miles. About 2 miles beyond this, the Lost Valley Road intersects the PCT (5.2 miles beyond the pavement). The trail to Combs Peak takes off to the left, heading north.

To find the trailhead for the Northern segment, begin at the fire station in the town of Anza. Drive 1 mile east on California Highway 371, turn right (south) on Kirby Road, then drive 1.1 miles to Wellman Road. (The road names change, but simply follow the paved road). Turn left on Wellman Road and proceed 1 mile to Terwilliger Road. Go right (south) on Terwilliger Road for 3 miles to Coyote Canyon Road, turn left, and continue 1.9 miles to a T intersection. Turn right toward the signed Coyote Canyon dirt road (pavement ends here) and follow the main dirt road 2.1 miles to the UPPER COYOTE CANYON ROAD sign on a hill. Park here and walk about 0.1 mile down rough Coyote Canyon Road to the PCT road crossing. The trail to Table Mountain takes off to the left, heading north.

The Hike

Anza-Borrego contains six long segments of the Pacific Crest Trail (PCT), which are separated from one another by major road crossings or by stretches of the trail that extend outside the park boundary. It is the opinion of the authors that the four park segments of the PCT from Pioneer Mail north to the Lost Valley Road run too close to major roads for quality backcountry hiking or are too long and dry for most destination-oriented day hikers. In contrast, the two remote northern segments presented here are split only by the rough Coyote Canyon Road, offering varied hiking opportunities in a scenic region of higher mountains and deep canyons.

The Pacific Crest Trail meets Lost Valley Road, south of Combs Peak.

The two PCT hikes described below are presented together because they are in close proximity along what is essentially the same stretch of the PCT. With a car shuttle it would be possible to take a 12-mile point-to-point day hike from Lost Valley Road north to Coyote Canyon Road, which is the takeoff point for the out-and-back hike north to Table Mountain.

Southern Segment

The PCT trailhead on the Lost Valley Road is 2 miles east of the park boundary sign. The PCT road crossing is faintly marked on a wooden post, along with a RIVERSIDE COUNTY LINE 6 sign. From the road, hike left (north) on the PCT, which maintains a moderate grade along the eastern slopes of Bucksnort Mountain. After 1.9 miles of climbing along the steep side slopes, the trail comes to a small level saddle at 5,595 feet to the immediate northeast of Combs Peak—the apex of Bucksnort Mountain. Pause among the Coulter pines here for a 180-degree view from lofty San Gorgonio Mountain to the north to the stark crest of the Santa Rosa Mountains and Salton Sea eastward. Coulter pine is also called "big-cone pine," and no wonder. It displays

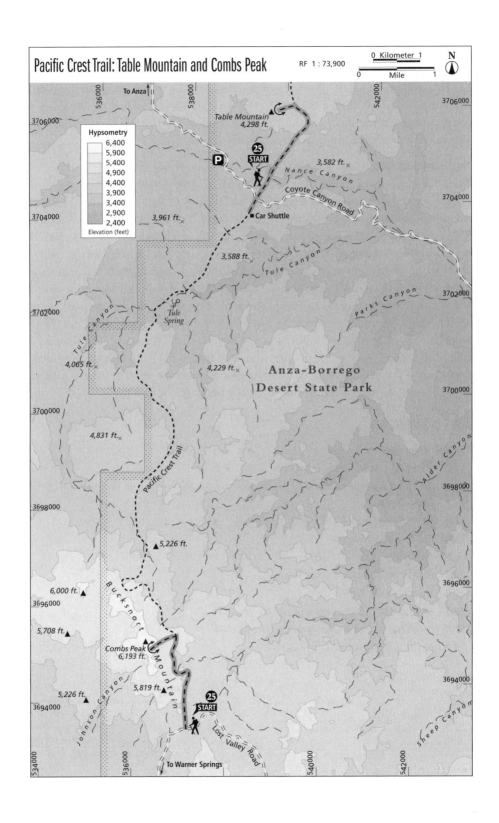

Pacific Crest Trail: Table Mountain and Combs Peak

RF 1 : 73,900

0 Kilometer 1

0 Mile 1

N

Hypsometry

| 6,400 |
| 5,900 |
| 5,400 |
| 4,900 |
| 4,400 |
| 3,900 |
| 3,400 |
| 2,900 |
| 2,400 |

Elevation (feet)

To Anza

Table Mountain
4,298 ft.

P

25 START

3,582 ft.×

Nance Canyon

Coyote Canyon Road

Car Shuttle

3,961 ft.×

3,588 ft.×

Tule Canyon

Parks Canyon

Tule Spring

Tule Canyon

4,065 ft.×

4,229 ft.×

Anza-Borrego Desert State Park

4,831 ft.×

Pacific Crest Trail

Alder Canyon

▲5,226 ft.

6,000 ft.▲

Bucksnort

5,708 ft.▲

Combs Peak
6,193 ft. ▲

Mountain

5,819 ft.▲

25 START

5,226 ft.▲

Johnson Canyon

Lost Valley Road

Sheep Canyon

To Warner Springs

536000 538000 540000 542000 534000 536000 540000 542000

3706000 3704000 3702000 3700000 3698000 3696000 3694000

the heaviest cones of all pine species on the planet—each cone weighing in at four to five pounds!

To expand the field of view from 180 to 360 degrees, climb southeasterly to the summit of Combs Peak, gaining 600 feet in 0.6 mile. Route-finding through dense brush is required, but the view alone makes the effort worthwhile. Return the way you came to complete this 5-mile round-trip sampler of the PCT.

Northern Segment

From the crest of the hill at the UPPER COYOTE CANYON ROAD sign near the park boundary gate, walk down the rough four-wheel-drive Coyote Canyon Road about 0.1 mile to its intersection with the PCT. This stretch of the PCT is also part of the California Riding and Hiking Trail. Take the trail to the left (north), which is marked by a mountain-lion-warning sign. The trail descends a gully, switchbacks once, then drops to the grassy bottom of colorful Nance Canyon. A gradual grade wraps around a low knoll, then crosses a rugged slope that provides vistas to the east and south of Coyote and other secluded canyons in the wild northern reaches of the park.

The trail continues climbing to a 4,185-foot brush-covered notch on Table Mountain. The actual summit of the broad expanse of the mountain is only a 0.2-mile, 110-foot off-trail climb to the west, less than 0.5 mile south of the north boundary of the park. Most of this 5-mile round-trip route crosses Bureau of Land Management sections of land included within the park's boundaries.

Miles and Directions

Southern segment:
- **0.0** Start at Lost Valley Road (5,050 feet).
- **1.9** Arrive at the saddle northeast of Combs Peak and the beginning of the off-trail climb to Combs Peak.
- **2.5** Reach Combs Peak (6,193 feet).
- **5.0** Return to the trailhead.

Northern segment:
- **0.0** Start at Upper Coyote Canyon Road.
- **0.3** Arrive at Nance Canyon.
- **2.3** Arrive at a 4,185-foot pass east of Table Mountain.
- **2.5** Reach the summit of Table Mountain (4,298 feet).
- **5.0** Return to the trailhead.

Afterword

As seasoned hikers accustomed to the high snowy mountains of the Northern Rockies, we were excited when the idea of exploring some of the California desert was presented to us. It would be hard to find two more disparate regions—the California desert and the Northern Rockies—within the lower forty-eight. We viewed the opportunity to learn more about such a different ecosystem as a tremendous challenge. And we foresaw many interim challenges along the way, such as the challenge of truly getting to know this splendid country and its hidden treasures beyond the roads. There would be the challenges of climbing rugged peaks, of safely traversing vast expanses of open desert, of navigating across alluvial fans to secluded canyons, of learning enough about the interconnected web of desert geology, flora, and fauna to be able to interpret some of its wonders for others to appreciate. These beckoned to us from blank spots on the park map.

But we each face a far greater challenge: the challenge of wilderness stewardship, which must be shared by all who venture into the wilderness of Anza-Borrego and California's other desert parks.

Wilderness stewardship can take many forms, from political advocacy to a zero-impact hiking and camping ethic to quietly setting the example of respect for wild country for others to follow. The political concessions that eventually brought about passage of the long-awaited California Desert Protection Act have been made. Boundaries were gerrymandered, exclusions made, and nonconforming uses grandfathered. Still, the park lines that have been drawn for this great park represent a tremendous step forward in the ongoing battle to save what little remains of our diminishing wilderness heritage.

But drawing lines is only the first step. Now, the great challenge is to take care of what we have. We can each demonstrate this care every time we set out on a hike. It comes down to respect for the untamed but fragile desert, for those wild creatures who have no place else to live, for other visitors, and for those yet unborn who will retrace our hikes into the next century and beyond.

We will be judged not by the mountains we climb but by what we pass on to others in an unimpaired condition. Happy hiking, and may your trails be clear with the wind and sun at your back.

Appendix A: Our Favorite Hikes

Open Desert

Alcoholic Pass (20) Alluvial fan and ridge climb to low mountain pass

Waterfall and Stream

Sheep Canyon (24) Mountain valley with stream and fan palms

Oases

Mountain Palm Springs Loop (1) Series of palm groves, largest group of California fan palms
Borrego Palm Canyon Nature Trail (19) Falls, palm oasis in steep canyon

Interpretive Nature Trail

Borrego Palm Canyon Nature Trail (19) Excellent plant identification/bighorn-sheep country

Prehistory and History

The Morteros (8) Native American sites
Pictograph Trail (9) Native American sites

Appendix B: Recommended Equipment

Use the following checklists as you assemble your gear for hiking Anza-Borrego Desert Park.

Day Hike

- ❏ sturdy, well-broken-in, light- to medium-weight hiking boots
- ❏ broad-brimmed hat, which must be windproof
- ❏ long-sleeved shirt for sun protection
- ❏ long pants for protection against sun and brush
- ❏ water: two quarts to one gallon/day (depending on season), in sturdy screw-top plastic containers
- ❏ large-scale topo map and compass (adjusted for magnetic declination)
- ❏ whistle, mirror, and matches (for emergency signals)
- ❏ flashlight (in case your hike takes longer than you expect)
- ❏ sunblock and lip sunscreen
- ❏ insect repellent (in season)
- ❏ pocketknife
- ❏ small first-aid kit: tweezers, bandages, antiseptic, moleskin, snakebite extractor kit
- ❏ bee sting kit (over-the-counter antihistamine or epinephrine by prescription) as needed for the season
- ❏ windbreaker (or rain gear in season)
- ❏ lunch or snack, with baggie for your trash
- ❏ toilet paper, with a plastic zipper bag to pack it out
- ❏ your FalconGuide

Optional gear
- ❏ camera and film
- ❏ binoculars
- ❏ bird and plant guidebooks
- ❏ notebook and pen/pencil

Winter High-Country Trips

All of the above, plus:
- ❏ gaiters
- ❏ warm ski-type hat and gloves
- ❏ warm jacket

Backpacking Trips/Overnights

All of the above, plus:

- ❏ backpack (internal or external frame)
- ❏ more water (at least a gallon a day, plus extra for cooking—cache or carry)
- ❏ clothing for the season
- ❏ sleeping bag and pad
- ❏ tent with fly
- ❏ toiletries
- ❏ stove with fuel bottle and repair kit
- ❏ pot, bowl, cup, and eating utensils
- ❏ food (freeze-dried meals require extra water)
- ❏ water filter designed and approved for backcountry use (if the route passes a water source)
- ❏ nylon cord (50 to 100 feet for hanging food, drying clothes, etc.)
- ❏ additional plastic bags for carrying out trash

Appendix C: Other Information Sources and Maps

Natural History Association

Anza-Borrego Desert Natural History Association
652 Palm Canyon Drive
Borrego Springs, CA 92004
(760) 767–3052/3098
E-mail: ABDNHA@uia.net
Web site: www.abdnha.org

This nonprofit membership organization is dedicated to the preservation and interpretation of the natural and human history of Anza-Borrego Desert State Park. Membership benefits include book discounts, educational programs, and periodic newsletters.

Other Handy Maps

Although the "At a Glance" chart lists only the detailed 7.5-minute topographic maps for each hike, the natural history association also sells additional maps that are indispensable for overall trip planning and for navigating around the park to and between hikes.

Anza-Borrego Desert State Park

- Anza-Borrego Desert Region Recreation Map (color)
- Topographic map set of eight 15-minute black-and-white maps covering the entire park, published by the Anza-Borrego Desert Natural History Association
- AAA map of San Diego County published by the Automobile Club of Southern California

Appendix D: Park Management Agencies

District Superintendent
Anza-Borrego Desert State Park
200 Palm Canyon Drive
Borrego Springs, CA 92004
Park information and administrative office, (760) 767–5311
Camping reservations, Destinet, (800) 444–7275
Web site: www.anzaborrego.statepark.org

Agua Caliente County Park (surrounded by Anza-Borrego DSP)
c/o San Diego County Parks and Recreation Department
5201 Ruffin Road, Suite P
San Diego, CA 92123
Information, (760) 694–3049
Campground reservations, (760) 565–3600

For information about wilderness and other public lands adjacent to the park, contact:
Bureau of Land Management
California Desert District
6221 Box Springs Boulevard
Riverside, CA 92507
(951) 697–5200
Web site: www.californiadesert.gov

Index

About the Authors

Polly and Bill Cunningham are married partners on the long trail of life. Polly, formerly a history teacher in St. Louis, Missouri, now makes her home with Bill in Choteau, Montana. She is pursuing multiple careers as a freelance writer and wilderness guide and working with the elderly. Polly has hiked and backpacked extensively throughout many parts of the country.

Bill is a lifelong "Wildernut," as a conservation activist, backpacking outfitter, and former wilderness field studies instructor. During the 1970s and 1980s he was a field rep for The Wilderness Society and Montana Wilderness Association. Bill has written several books, including *Wild Montana,* published by Falcon Press in 1995, plus numerous articles about wilderness areas based on his extensive personal exploration.

In addition to *Hiking Anza-Borrego Desert State Park,* Polly and Bill have co-authored several other FalconGuide books, including *Wild Utah* (1998), *Hiking New Mexico's Gila Wilderness* (1999), *Hiking New Mexico's Aldo Leopold Wilderness* (2002), and *Hiking California's Desert Parks* (2006).

Decades ago both Bill and Polly lived in California close to the desert—Bill in Bakersfield and Polly in San Diego. They enjoyed renewing their ties with California while exploring the Anza-Borrego region for this book. Months of driving, camping, and hiking, with laptop and camera, have increased their enthusiasm for California's desert wilderness. They want others to have as much fun exploring this fabulously wide-open country as they had.

Authors Polly and Bill Cunningham